P9-DUI-197

HARRAP'S

Spanish

PHRASE BOOK

Compiled by
LEXUS

with

Carmen Alonso-Bartol de Billinghurst

HARRAP

EDINBURGH
NEW YORK   TORONTO

Distributed in the United States by

PRENTICE HALL
New York

First published in Great Britain 1988
by HARRAP BOOKS Ltd
43–45 Annandale Street, Edinburgh EH7 4AZ

ISBN 0 245-54663-4
In the United States, ISBN 0-13-383183-2

Reprinted 1988 *and* 1989 *(three times)*, 1992

Library of Congress Cataloging-in-Publication Data

Harrap's Spanish phrase book / compiled by Lexus with Carmen
Alonso – Bartol de Billinghurst.
p.   cm.
English and Spanish.
"First published in Great Britain, 1988" – T.p. verso.
ISBN 0-13-383183-3 (Prentice Hall)
1. Spanish language – Conversation and phrase books. I. Alonso –
Bartol de Billinghurst, Carmen. II Lexus (Firm)
PC4121.H423 1990   89-48978
468.3'421 – dc20   CIP

Printed in England by Clays Ltd, St Ives plc

CONTENTS

The phrase sections in this new book are concise and to the point. In each section you will find: a list of basic vocabulary; a selection of useful phrases; a list of common words and expressions that you will see on signs and notices. A full pronunciation guide is given for things you'll want to say or ask and typical replies to some of your questions are listed.

Of course, there are bound to be occasions when you want to know more. So this book allows for this by containing a two-way Spanish-English dictionary with a total of some 5,000 references. This will enable you to build up your Spanish vocabulary, to make variations on the phrases in the phrase sections and to recognize more of the Spanish words that you will see or hear when travelling about.

As well as this we have given a menu reader covering about 200 dishes and types of food — so that you will know what you are ordering! And, as a special feature, there is a section on colloquial Spanish.

Speaking the language can make all the difference to your trip. So:

buena suerte!
bwena swairteh
good luck!

and

buen viaje!
bwen bee-aнeh
have a good trip!

5

PRONUNCIATION

In the phrase sections of this book a pronunciation guide has been given by writing the Spanish words as though they were English. So if you read out the pronunciation as English words a Spanish person should be able to understand you. Some notes on this:

'eye' the quote marks mean pronounce this as the English word 'eye'.

ow is pronounced as in 'cow'.

H is a sound made at the back of the throat and is similar to the 'ch' sound when a Scotsman says 'loch'.

Letters in bold type in the pronunciation guide mean that this part of the word should be stressed.

GENERAL PHRASES

hello, hi
hola
ola

good morning
buenos días
bwenoss dee-ass

good evening
buenas tardes
bwenass tardess

good night
buenas noches
bwenass nochess

pleased to meet you
encantado (de conocerle)
enkantado (deh konothairleh)

goodbye, cheerio
adiós
ad-yoss

see you
hasta luego
asta lwehgo

yes
sí
see

no
no
no

yes please
sí, por favor
see por fabor

GENERAL PHRASES

no thank you
no, gracias
no grath-yass

please
por favor
por fabor

thank you/ thanks
gracias
grath-yass

thanks very much
muchas gracias
moochass grath-yass

you're welcome
de nada
deh nada

sorry
perdone
pairdoneh

sorry? (*didn't understand*)
¿cómo dice?
komo deetheh

how are you?
¿qué tal está?
keh tal esta

very well, thank you
muy bien, gracias
mwee b-yen grath-yass

and yourself?
¿y usted?
ee oosteh

excuse me! (*to get attention*)
¡oiga!
oyga

how much is it?
¿cuánto es?
kwanto ess

GENERAL PHRASES

can I ...?
¿puedo ...?
pwehdo

can I have ...?
quisiera ...
keesee-ehra

I'd like to ...
quisiera ...
keesee-ehra

where is ...?
¿dónde está ...?
dondeh esta

it's not ...
no es/ está ...
no ess/ esta

is it ...?
¿es/ está ...?
ess/ esta

is there ... here?
¿hay ... aquí?
'eye' ... akee

could you say that again?
¿puede repetir?
pweh-deh reh-peh-teer

please don't speak so fast
¿podría hablar más despacio?
podree-a ablar mass despath-yo

I don't understand
no entiendo
no entee-endo

OK
vale
baleh

come on, let's go!
¡vámonos!
bamonoss

GENERAL PHRASES

wait for me!
¡espéreme!
espeh-reh-meh

what's your name?
¿cómo se llama?
komo seh yama

what's that in Spanish?
¿cómo se dice eso en español?
komo seh deetheh esso en espan-yol

that's fine!
está bien
esta b-yen

abierto	open
aseos	toilets
caballeros	gents
cerrado	closed
damas	ladies
empujar	push
llame antes de entrar	knock before entering
oficina de información y turismo	tourist information office
papelera	litter
prohibida la entrada	no entry
prohibido	forbidden
prohibido fijar carteles	stick no bills
recién pintado	wet paint
se ruega . . .	please . . .
se ruega no . . .	please do not . . .
se vende	for sale
servicios	toilets
señoras	ladies
sírvase . . .	please . . .
tirar	pull

COMING AND GOING

airport	el aeropuerto	*a-ehropwairto*
baggage	el equipaje	*ekeepaнeh*
book (*in advance*)	reservar	*rehsairbar*
coach	un autobús	*owtobooss*
docks	el muelle	*mweh-yeh*
ferry	el ferry	*fairree*
gate (*at airport*)	la puerta	*pwairta*
harbour	el puerto	*pwairto*
plane	el avión	*ab-yon*
sleeper	una litera	*leetaira*
station	la estación	*estath-yon*
taxi	un taxi	*taksee*
terminal	la terminal	*tairmeenal*
train	el tren	*tren*

a ticket to ...
un billete para ...
oon beel-yehteh para

I'd like to reserve a seat
quisiera reservar un asiento
keesee-ehra rehsairbar oon ass-yento

smoking/ non-smoking please
fumadores/ no fumadores, por favor
foomadoress/ no foomadoress por fabor

a window seat, please
un asiento cerca de la ventana, por favor
oon ass-yento thairka deh la bentana por fabor

which platform is it for ...?
¿de qué andén sale el tren para ...?
deh keh anden saleh el tren para

what time is the next flight?
¿a qué hora sale el próximo vuelo?
a keh ora saleh el prokseemo bwehlo

11

COMING AND GOING

is this the right train for . . .?
¿es éste el tren para . . .?
ess esteh el tren para

is this bus going to . . .?
¿es éste el autobús que va a . . .?
ess esteh el owtobooss keh ba a

is this seat free?
¿está libre este asiento?
esta leebreh esteh ass-yento

do I have to change (trains)?
¿tengo que hacer transbordo?
teng-go keh athair transbordo

is this the right stop for . . .?
¿es ésta la parada para . . .?
ess esta la parada para

which terminal is it for . . .?
¿cuál es la terminal para . . .?
kwal ess la tairmeenal para

is this ticket OK?
¿vale este billete?
baleh esteh beel-yehteh

I want to change my ticket
quisiera cambiar mi billete
keesee-ehra kamb-yar mee beel-yehteh

thanks for a lovely stay
gracias por su hospitalidad
grath-yass por soo ospeetaleeda

thanks very much for coming to meet me
muchas gracias por venir a esperarme
moochass grath-yass por behneer a espehrarmeh

well, here we are in . . .
bueno, ya estamos en . . .
bweno ya estamoss en

COMING AND GOING

¿tiene algo que declarar?
t-yeneh algo keh dehklarar
do you have anything to declare?

¿podría abrir su maleta, por favor?
podree-a abreer soo malehta por fabor
would you mind opening this bag
please?

abróchense los cinturones	fasten your seat belts
aduana	customs
alquiler de coches	car rental
andén	platform
billetes	tickets
circule por la derecha	keep right
consigna	left luggage
control de pasaportes	passport control
entrada	entrance
equipaje de mano	hand luggage
estación de trenes	railway station
firme deslizante	slippery road surface
fumadores	smoking
llegadas	arrivals
no fumadores	no smoking
puerta	gate
recogida de equipajes	baggage claim
retraso	delay
sala de embarque	departure room
sala de espera	waiting room
salida	exit
salidas	departures
tarjeta de embarque	boarding card

GETTING A ROOM

balcony	un balcón *balkon*
bed	una cama *kama*
breakfast	el desayuno *dessa-yoono*
dining room	el comedor *komehdor*
dinner	la cena *thehna*
double room	una habitación doble *abeetath-yon dobleh*
guesthouse	la pensión *pens-yon*
hotel	el hotel *otel*
key	la llave *yabeh*
lunch	el almuerzo *almwairtho*
night	una noche *nocheh*
private bathroom	un cuarto de baño privado *kwarto deh ban-yo preebado*
reception	la recepción *reh-thepth-yon*
room	una habitación *abeetath-yon*
shower	una ducha *doocha*
single room	una habitación individual *abeetath-yon eendeebeedoo-al*
with bath	con baño *kon ban-yo*
youth hostel	un albergue de juventud *albairgeh deh ноobentoo*

do you have a room for one night?
quisiera una habitación para una noche
keesee-ehra oona abeetath-yon para oona nocheh

do you have a room for one person?
quisiera una habitación individual
keesee-ehra oona abeetath-yon eendeebeedoo-al

do you have a room for two people?
quisiera una habitación doble
keesee-ehra oona abeetath-yon dobleh

we'd like to rent a room for a week
quisiéramos alquilar una habitación para una semana
keesee-ehramoss alkeelar oona abeetath-yon para oona semana

GETTING A ROOM

I'm looking for a good cheap room
estoy buscando una buena habitación que no sea cara
estoy booskando oona bwehna abeetath-yon keh no seh-a kara

I have a reservation
he hecho una reserva
eh echo oona rehsairba

how much is it?
¿cuánto cuesta la habitación?
kwanto kwesta la abeetath-yon

can I see the room please?
¿podría ver la habitación, por favor?
podree-a bair la abeetath-yon por fabor

does that include breakfast?
¿está incluido el desayuno en el precio?
esta eenkloo-eedo el dessa-yoono en el preth-yo

a room overlooking the sea
una habitación con vistas al mar
oona abeetath-yon kon beestass al mar

we'd like to stay another night
quisiéramos quedarnos otra noche
keesee-ehramoss kehdarnoss otra nocheh

we will be arriving late
llegaremos tarde por la noche
yehgarehmoss tardeh por la nocheh

can I have my bill please?
por favor, ¿podría prepararme la cuenta?
por fabor podree-a prehpararmeh la kwenta

I'll pay cash
pagaré en efectivo
pagareh en efekteebo

can I pay by credit card?
¿aceptan tarjetas de crédito?
atheptan tarнehtass deh kredeeto

GETTING A ROOM

will you give me a call at 6.30 in the morning?
¿podrían despertarme a las 6 y media de la mañana?
podree-an despairtarmeh a lass sehss ee mehdee-a deh la man-yana

at what time do you serve breakfast/ dinner?
¿a qué hora se sirve el desayuno/ la cena?
a keh ora seh seerbeh el dessa-yoono/ la thehna

can we have breakfast in our room?
¿podrían traernos el desayuno a la habitación?
podree-an tra-airnoss el dessa-yoono a la abeetath-yon

thanks for putting us up
gracias por la cama
grath-yass por la kama

albergue de juventud	youth hostel
almuerzo	lunch
ascensor	lift
CH	guesthouse
comedor	dining room
completo	no vacancies
ducha	shower
media pensión	half board
pensión	guesthouse
piso bajo	ground floor
planta baja	ground floor
primer piso	first floor
salida de emergencia	fire escape
se alquilan habitaciones	rooms to rent
se ruega desalojen su habitación antes de las doce	please vacate your room by 12 noon
se ruega no molestar	please do not disturb
segundo piso	second floor
sótano	basement

EATING OUT

bill	la cuenta *kwenta*
dessert	el postre *postreh*
drink	beber *bebair*
eat	comer *komair*
food	la comida *komeeda*
main course	el segundo plato *segoondo plato*
menu	el menú *menoo*
restaurant	el restaurante *restowranteh*
salad	la ensalada *ensalada*
service	el servicio *sairbeeth-yo*
starter	el primer plato *preemair plato*
tip	la propina *propeena*
waiter	el camarero *kamarehro*
waitress	la camarera *kamarehra*

a table for three, please
una mesa para tres, por favor
oona messa para tress por fabor

can I see the menu?
quisiera ver el menú
keesee-ehra bair el menoo

we'd like to order
quisiéramos pedir
keesee-ehramoss pehdeer

what do you recommend?
¿qué nos recomienda?
keh noss rekom-yenda

I'd like ... please
por favor, quisiera ...
por fabor keesee-ehra

waiter!
¡camarero!
kamarehro

17

EATING OUT

waitress!
¡camarera!
kamarehra

could we have the bill, please?
la cuenta, por favor
la kwenta por fabor

two white coffees please
dos cafés con leche, por favor
doss kafehss kon lecheh por fabor

that's for me
eso es para mí
esso ess para mee

some more bread please
un poco más de pan por favor
oon poko mass deh pan por fabor

a bottle of red/ white wine please
una botella de vino tinto/ blanco, por favor
oona botel-ya deh beeno teento/ blanko por fabor

auto-servicio	self-service
caballeros	gents
cafetería	café
comidas para llevar	take-away meals
menú del día	today's set menu
menú turístico	set menu
platos combinados	meat and vegetables, hamburgers and eggs etc *(normally if you order steak, for example, you'll get just a steak)*
señoras	ladies
servicio (no) incluido	service charge (not) included
tapas	small snacks

aceitunas negras/verdes black/green olives
aguacate avocado
agua mineral con gas/sin gas fizzy/still mineral water
ahumados smoked fish
albóndigas meat balls
alcachofas (con jamón) artichokes (with ham)
almejas a la marinera clams in wine and parsley
almejas al natural live clams
alubias beans
ancas de rana frogs' legs
anchoas anchovies
anguila (ahumada) (smoked) eel
angulas baby eels
apio celery
arenque herring
arroz rice
arroz con leche rice pudding
asado de ... roast ...
atún tuna
bacalao (al pil pil) cod (with chillies and garlic)
batido de ... ... milkshake
berenjenas aubergines
besugo bream
bistec de ternera veal steak
bizcocho de ... ... sponge
bocadillo de ... ... sandwich
bogavante lobster
bonito tuna
boquerones fritos/en vinagre fried anchovies/
  anchovies in vinaigrette
brazo de gitano Swiss roll
buñuelos light fried pastry
butifarra Catalan sausage
cabrito asado roast kid
calamares fritos/a la romana fried squid/squid rings in
  batter

MENU READER

calamares en su tinta squid in a black sauce
caldo clear soup
caldo gallego vegetable soup
callos a la madrileña tripe with chillies
camarones baby prawns
cangrejos (de río) (river) crabs
caracoles snails
carbonada de buey beef cooked in beer
carnes meat
carro de queso cheese board
centollo spider crab
champiñones mushrooms
chanfaina rice with fried blood
chanquetes whitebait
chipirones baby squid
chuleta de buey/cerdo/cordero/ternera
   beef/pork/lamb/veal chop
chuletitas de cordero small lamb chops
chuletón de buey/ternera large beef/veal chop
churros fried pastry cut into lengths
cigalas crayfish/langoustines
cochinillo asado roast sucking pig
cocido madrileño stew with chickpeas, pork, chicken
   and vegetables
cocochas (de merluza) throat of hake cooked with
   garlic and parsley
cóctel de gambas/mariscos prawn/seafood cocktail
codornices quail
coles de Bruselas Brussels sprouts
coliflor cauliflower
conejo asado/estofado roast/stewed rabbit
consomé (al jerez) consommé (with sherry)
cordero asado roast lamb
cordero chilindrón lamb stew with onions, tomatoes,
   peppers and egg
costillas de cerdo pork ribs
crema catalana crème brûlée (cream dessert with
   caramelized sugar)
crema de cangrejos/espárragos cream of
   crab/asparagus soup
criadillas de ternera veal testicles

MENU READER

criadillas de tierra ground tubers
crocante ice cream with chopped nuts
croquetas de ... ... croquettes
embutidos pork cured sausages
empanada gallega fish pie
empanadillas small pies
ensalada de fruta/pollo fruit/chicken salad
ensalada mixta mixed salad
ensaladilla (rusa) (Russian) salad with mayonnaise
entrecot a la parrilla grilled entrecôte steak
entremeses hors d'oeuvres
escabeche de ... marinated ...
escalope a la milanesa breaded veal with cheese
escalope de ternera/cerdo veal/pork escalope
espaguetis spaghetti
espárragos asparagus
espinacas a la crema creamed spinach
estofado de ... ... stew
fabada bean stew with sausage
faisán pheasant
filete de cerdo/ternera pork/veal steak
flan cream caramel
fresas (con nata) strawberries (with cream)
fruta fruit
gambas a la plancha/al ajillo grilled prawns/ prawns
  with garlic
gambas rebozadas prawns in batter
garbanzos chick peas
gazpacho andaluz cold vegetable soup
gazpacho manchego rabbit stew with tomato and
  garlic
guisantes con jamón peas with ham
helado de chocolate chocolate ice cream
helado de fresa strawberry ice cream
helado de mantecado vanilla ice cream
hígado liver
higos figs
huevos cocidos hard boiled eggs
huevos escalfados poached eggs
huevos fritos (con jamón) fried eggs (with ham)
huevos pasados por agua boiled eggs

MENU READER

huevos revueltos scrambled eggs
jamón York/serrano boiled/cured ham
jarra de vino jug of wine
jeta pig's cheek
judías (verdes) (green) beans
jugo de naranja/piña/tomate orange/pineapple/tomato juice
langosta lobster
langostinos a la plancha grilled king prawns
lengua de cerdo/cordero pork/lamb tongue
lenguado a la plancha/a la romana grilled/fried sole
lentejas lentils
licores liqueurs
liebre estofada stewed hare
lubina al horno baked sea bass
macarrones macaroni
manos de cerdo pigs' trotters
mantequilla butter
manzanas asadas baked apples
manzanilla camomile tea
mariscos seafood
mejillones a la marinera mussels in wine sauce with garlic and parsley
melocotón en almíbar peaches in syrup
melón (con jamón) melon (with ham)
menestra de legumbres/verdura vegetable stew
menú del día set menu
merluza a la plancha grilled hake
merluza a la romana hake steaks in batter
merluza a la vasca hake with chilies and garlic
merluza en salsa verde hake in parsley and wine sauce
mermelada de naranja/limón orange/lemon marmalade
mermelada de fresas/melocotón strawberry/peach jam
mero grouper (*fish*)
mollejas de ternera veal sweetbreads
morcilla black pudding
morros de cerdo pigs' cheeks
naranja orange

natillas cold custard
orejas de cerdo pigs' ears
paella de mariscos/de pollo fried rice with shellfish/chicken
paella valenciana fried rice with various shellfish and chicken
pan bread
panceta bacon
parrillada de mariscos mixed grilled shellfish
pastel de ... ... pie/cake
patatas asadas roast potatoes
patatas bravas potatoes with cayenne sauce
patatas fritas chips
patatas fritas (en bolsa) crisps
pato a la naranja duck à l'orange
pavo relleno stuffed turkey
pechugas de pollo chicken breasts
pepinillos gherkins
pepino cucumber
percebes goose barnacles (shellfish)
perdices partridges
pescado fish
pimientos fritos/rellenos fried/stuffed peppers
piña pineapple
pinchos morunos kebabs
pisto stewed marrow with onions and tomato
plátanos bananas
pollo al ajillo fried chicken with garlic
pollo asado roast chicken
polvorones sugar-based sweet eaten at Christmas
pulpo octopus
puré de patatas potato purée
queso cheese
quisquillas shrimps
rábanos radish
ración de ... portion of ...
remolacha beetroot
requesón cottage cheese
revuelto de ajos/angulas/gambas scrambled eggs with garlic/baby eels/prawns
riñones al jerez kidneys with sherry

MENU READER

rodaballo turbot
salchichas sausages
salchichón cured white sausage with pepper
salmón ahumado smoked salmon
salmonetes red mullet
salsa de ... ... sauce
sandía water melon
sangría mixture of red wine, orange and fruit
sardinas a la brasa barbecued sardines
sesos brains
shangurro spider crab cooked in shell
solomillo de ternera/cerdo fillet of veal /pork
sopa de ajo/legumbres/mariscos
  garlic/vegetables/shellfish soup
tarta de chocolate/fresas chocolate/strawberry cake
tarta de manzana apple pie
tarta helada ice cream gateau
ternera veal
tomates tomatoes
tortilla a su gusto omelette made as the customer
  wishes
tortilla francesa/de patatas plain/potato omelette
tostón sucking pig
trucha trout
vaca estofada stewed beef
vieiras scallops
zarzuela de mariscos shellfish stew
zumo de naranja/limón orange/lemon juice

HAVING A DRINK

bar	un bar	*bar*
beer	una cerveza	*thairbeh-tha*
closing time	la hora de cerrar	*ora deh thairrar*
coke (R)	una coca-cola	*koka-kola*
dry	seco	*seko*
fresh orange	un zumo de naranja	*thoomo deh naranна*
gin and tonic	una ginebra con tónica	*нeenehbra kon toneeka*
ice	el hielo	*yehlo*
lager	una cerveza	*thairbeh-tha*
lemonade	una limonada	*leemonada*
pub	un bar	*bar*
red	tinto	*teento*
straight	solo	*solo*
sweet	dulce	*dooltheh*
vodka	un vodka	*bodka*
whisky	un whisky	*weeskee*
white	blanco	*blanko*
wine	el vino	*beeno*

let's go for a drink
vamos a tomar una copa
bamoss a tomar oona kopa

a beer please
una cerveza, por favor
oona thairbeh-tha por fabor

two beers please
dos cervezas, por favor
doss thairbeh-thass por fabor

a glass of red/ white wine
un vaso de vino tinto/ blanco
oon basso deh beeno teento/ blanko

25

HAVING A DRINK

with lots of ice
con mucho hielo
kon moocho yehlo

no ice, thanks
sin hielo, por favor
seen yehlo por fabor

can I have another one?
¿me trae otro?
meh tra-eh otro

the same again please
lo mismo, por favor
lo meesmo por fabor

what'll you have?
¿qué vas a tomar?
keh bass a tomar

I'll get this round
yo pago esta ronda
yo pago esta ronda

not for me thanks
para mí no, gracias
para mee no grath-yass

he's absolutely smashed
está completamente bebido
esta kompletamenteh bebeedo

café con leche	white coffee (*large cup*)
café cortado	white coffee (*small cup*)
café solo	black coffee
caña	small glass of beer
cervecería	bar
cerveza	lager
cerveza de barril	draught beer
lista de precios	price list
té con limón	lemon tea
vino blanco/tinto	white/red wine

COLLOQUIAL EXPRESSIONS

barmy	chalado *chalado*
bastard	cabrón *kabron*
bird	una chica *cheeka*
bloke	un tío *tee-o*
boozer (*pub*)	un bar *bar*
nutter	un loco *loko*
pissed	borracho *borracho*
thickie	un tonto/ una tonta *tonto, tonta*
twit	un/ una imbécil *eembeh-theel*

great!
¡estupendo!
estoopendo

that's awful!
¡qué horror!
keh orror

shut up!
¡cállate!
ka-yateh

ouch!
¡ay!
'eye'

yum-yum!
¡qué rico!
keh reeko

I'm absolutely knackered
estoy agotado
estoy agotado

I'm fed up
estoy harto
estoy arto

COLLOQUIAL EXPRESSIONS

I'm fed up with ...
estoy harto de ...
estoy arto deh

don't make me laugh!
¡no me hagas reír!
no meh agass reh-eer

you've got to be joking!
¡no digas bobadas!
no deegass bobadass

it's rubbish (*goods etc*)
es malísimo
ess maleesseemo

it's a rip-off
es un robo
ess oon robo

get lost!
¡márchese!
marchehseh

it's a nuisance
¡qué pesadez!
keh pehsadeth

it's absolutely fantastic
es estupendo
ess estoopendo

de acuerdo	it's OK
dominguero!	learn to drive!
eso es	that's it
estupendo	great
¡hombre!	*expresses surprise, anger or pleasure*
no puedo creerlo	I don't believe it
tonto	silly
vale	OK

28

GETTING AROUND

bike	una bici *beethee*
bus	el autobús *owtobooss*
car	un coche *kocheh*
change (trains etc)	cambiar *kamb-yar*
garage (for fuel)	una gasolinera *gassoleenaira*
hitch-hike	hacer auto-stop *athair owtostop*
map	un mapa *mapa*
moped	una mobylette *mobeelehteh*
motorbike	una moto *moto*
petrol	la gasolina *la gassoleena*
return ticket	un billete de ida y vuelta *beel-yehteh deh eeda ee bwelta*
single	un billete de ida *beel-yehteh deh eeda*
station	la estación *estath-yon*
taxi	un taxi *taksee*
ticket	un billete *beel-yehteh*
train	el tren *tren*
underground	el metro *metro*

I'd like to rent a car/bicycle
quisiera alquilar un coche/una bicicleta
keesee-ehra alkeelar oon kocheh/ oona beethee-klehta

how much is it per day?
¿cuánto es por día?
kwanto ess por deea

when do I have to bring the car back?
¿cuándo tengo que devolver el coche?
kwando teng-go keh dehbolbair el kocheh

I'm heading for ...
voy a ...
boy a

GETTING AROUND

how do I get to . . . ?
¿para ir a . . . ?
para eer a

REPLIES   **todo recto**
tohdo rekto
straight on

tuerza a la izquierda/ derecha
twairtha a la eethk-yairda/ dehreh-cha
turn left/ right

es ese edificio de allí
ess esseh ehdeefeeth-yo deh a-yee
it's that building there

es por ese otro lado
ess por esseh otro lado
it's back that way

la primera/ segunda/ tercera a la izquierda
la preemaira/ segoonda/ tairthaira a la eethk-yairda
first/ second/ third on the left

we're just travelling around
estamos recorriendo la región
estamoss rekor-yendo la reh-нee-yon

I'm a stranger here
no soy de aquí
no soy deh akee

is that on the way?
¿está de camino?
esta deh kameeno

can I get off here?
¿puedo bajar aquí?
pwehdo baнar akee

thanks very much for the lift
gracias por traerme en el coche
grath-yass por tra-airmeh en el kocheh

two returns to . . . please
dos billetes de ida y vuelta para . . ., por favor
doss beel-yehtess deh eeda ee bwelta para . . . por fabor

what time is the last train back?
¿a qué hora vuelve el último tren?
a keh ora bwelbeh el oolteemo tren

we want to leave tomorrow and come back the day after
queremos salir mañana y volver al día siguiente
kerehmoss saleer man-yana ee bolbair al dee-a seeg-yenteh

we're coming back the same day
volveremos el mismo día
bolbairehmoss el meesmo dee-a

is this the right platform for . . .?
¿es éste el andén para ir a . . .?
ess esteh el anden para eer a

is this train going to . . .?
¿es éste el tren para . . .?
ess esteh el tren para

which station is this?
¿qué estación es ésta?
keh estath-yon ess esta

which stop is it for . . .?
¿dónde tengo que bajar para ir a . . .?
dondeh teng-go keh baнar para eer a

can I take my bike on the train?
¿puedo llevar la bici en el tren?
pwehdo yehbar la beethee en el tren

how far is it to the nearest petrol station?
¿a qué distancia está la gasolinera más próxima?
a keh deestanth-ya esta la gassoleenaira mass prokseema

I need a new tyre
necesito un neumático nuevo
netheseeto oon nehoomateeko nwehbo

it's overheating
el motor se calienta
el motor seh kal-yenta

GETTING AROUND

there's something wrong with the brakes
los frenos no funcionan bien
loss frehnoss no foonth-yonan b-yen

andén	platform
aparcamiento	car park
autopista	motorway
cambio de sentido	get in filter lane to turn off across flow of traffic
ceda el paso	give way
centro ciudad	town centre
curva peligrosa	dangerous bend
despacho de billetes	ticket office
desviación	diversion
dirección prohibida	no entry
dirección única	one way
estación de autobuses	bus station
estacionamiento limitado	restricted parking
llegadas	arrival(s)
metro	underground
normal	2 star petrol
obras	roadworks
peaje	toll
prioridad a la derecha	vehicles coming from the right have priority
prohibido aparcar	no parking
puente	bridge
salida de autopista	motorway exit
salidas	departure(s)
se ruega no aparcar	no parking please
super	4 star petrol
TALGO	fast luxury train
TER	express train
trenes de cercanías	suburban trains
zona azul	restricted parking area in town centre

SHOPPING

carrier bag	una bolsa *bolsa*
cashdesk	la caja *kaнa*
cheap	barato *barato*
cheque	un cheque *chekeh*
department	la sección *sekth-yon*
expensive	caro *karo*
pay	pagar *pagar*
receipt	un recibo *reh-theebo*
shop	una tienda *t-yenda*
shop assistant	el empleado *empleh-ado*
	la empleada *empleh-ada*
supermarket	el supermercado *soopairmairkado*
till	la caja *kaнa*

I'd like ...
quisiera ...
keesee-ehra

have you got ...?
¿tiene ...?
t-yeneh

how much is this?
¿cuánto es esto?
kwanto ess esto

can I just have a look around?
¿puedo mirar?
pwehdo meerar

the one in the window
el/ la de la ventana
el/ la deh la bentana

do you take credit cards?
¿aceptan tarjetas de crédito?
atheptan tarнehtass deh kredeeto

33

SHOPPING

could I have a receipt please?
¿podría darme un recibo?
podree-a darmeh oon reh-theebo

I'd like to try it on
quisiera probármelo
keesee-ehra probarmehlo

I'll come back
volveré
bolbaireh

it's too big/ small
es demasiado grande/ pequeño
ess demasseeado grandeh/ pehkehn-yo

it's not what I'm looking for
no es lo que estoy buscando
no ess lo keh estoy booskando

I'll take it
me lo llevo
meh lo yehbo

can you gift-wrap it?
¿puede envolvérmelo para regalo?
pwehdeh enbolbairmehlo para rehgalo

abierto	open
alimentación	food
caduca . . .	best before . . .
caja	till
cerrado	closed
consúmase antes de . . .	best before . . .
guárdese en sitio fresco	keep in a cool place
horario	opening times
IVA	VAT
rebajas	sale
se ruega pagar en caja	pay at the desk
vestuarios	changing room

SPAIN AND THINGS SPANISH

Some names which are different:

Balearic Islands	las Baleares *balay-aress*
Canaries	las Islas Canarias *eeslass kanaryass*
Castile	Castilla *kasteeya*
Catalonia	Cataluña *kataloonya*
Majorca	Mallorca *ma-yorka*
Pyrenees	los Pirineos *peereenay-oss*
la Alhambra	Moorish palace in Granada
el Ayuntamiento	town hall
benvengut	welcome (*in Catalan*)
castañuelas	castanets
castellano	Castillian; another word for the Spanish language
corrida de toros	bullfight
encierro	bull-running in Pamplona, the bulls loose in the streets
el Escorial	palace and convent near Madrid built in the second part of the 16th century
jerez	sherry (*pronounced:* Hair-eth)
oficina de turismo	tourist information office
plaza de toros	bullring
Plaza Mayor	Main Square
el Prado	art gallery in Madrid (*houses Picasso's Guernica*)
las Ramblas	picturesque street in Barcelona
el Rastro	open air market in Madrid
la Sagrada Familia	new cathedral in Barcelona built by Gaudí
San Fermín	July 7th, when the 'encierro' happens
Santiago	July 25th, a national holiday
Semana Santa	Easter Week, celebrated all over the country with religious processions
tancat	closed (*in Catalan*)
torero	bullfighter
toro	bull

MONEY

bank	un banco *banko*
bill	la cuenta *kwenta*
bureau de change	un cambio de moneda *kamb-yo deh monehda*
cash dispenser	un cajero automático *kaнehro owtomateeko*
change (*small*)	el cambio *el kamb-yo*
cheque	un cheque *chekeh*
credit card	una tarjeta de crédito *tarнehta deh kredeeto*
Eurocheque	un eurocheque *eh-oorochekeh*
exchange rate	el tipo de cambio *teepo deh kamb-yo*
expensive	caro *karo*
pounds (*sterling*)	las libras esterlinas *leebrass estairleenass*
price	el precio *preth-yo*
receipt	un recibo *reh-theebo*
Spanish pesetas	las pesetas españolas *pessehtass espan-yoless*
traveller's cheque	un cheque de viaje *chekeh deh b-yaнeh*

how much is it?
¿cuánto es?
kwanto ess

I'd like to change this into ...
quisiera cambiar esto en ...
keesee-ehra kamb-yar esto en

can you give me something smaller?
¿podría darme dinero suelto?
podree-a darmeh deenehro swelto

can I use this credit card?
¿aceptan esta tarjeta de crédito?
atheptan esta tarнehta deh kredeeto

MONEY

can we have the bill please?
la cuenta, por favor
la kwenta por fabor

please keep the change
quédese con la vuelta
kehdehseh kon la bwelta

does that include service?
¿está incluido el servicio?
esta eenkloo-eedo el sairbeeth-yo

what are your rates?
¿qué tarifa tienen?
keh tareefa t-yenen

I think the figures are wrong
creo que hay un error
kreh-o keh 'eye' oon airror

I'm completely skint
no tengo ni una perra
no teng-go nee oona pair-ra

The unit is the 'peseta' *pessayta*. Five pesetas is known colloquially as 'un duro' *dooro*.

banco	bank
caja	cashier (*the desk at which you get your money*)
caja de ahorros	savings bank
cajero automático	cash dispenser
cambio	exchange rate
cambio de moneda	exchange
compramos a . . .	buying rate
libra esterlina	pound sterling
tarjeta de crédito	credit card
vendemos a . . .	selling rate

ENTERTAINMENT

band (*pop*)	un conjunto *konнoonto*
cinema	el cine *theeneh*
concert	un concierto *konth-yairto*
disco	una discoteca *deeskotehka*
film	una película *pehleekoola*
go out	salir *saleer*
music	la música *mooseeka*
night out	una salida nocturna *saleeda noktoorna*
play (*theatre*)	una obra de teatro *obra deh teh-atro*
seat	un asiento *ass-yento*
show	un espectáculo *espektakoolo*
singer	un/ una cantante *kantanteh*
theatre	el teatro *teh-atro*
ticket	una entrada *entrada*

are you doing anything tonight?
¿qué vas a hacer esta noche?
keh bass a athair esta nocheh

do you want to come out with me tonight?
¿quieres salir conmigo, esta noche?
kee-ehress saleer konmeego esta nocheh

what's on?
¿qué ponen?
keh ponen

have you got a programme of what's on in town?
¿tienes un programa de espectáculos?
t-yeness oon programa deh espektakooloss

which is the best disco round here?
¿cuál es la mejor discoteca de por aquí?
kwal ess la meh-нor deeskotehka deh por akee

let's go to the cinema/ theatre
vamos al cine/ al teatro
bamoss al theeneh/ al teh-atro

ENTERTAINMENT

I've seen it
ya lo/ la he visto
ya lo/ la eh beesto

I'll meet you at 9 o'clock at the station
nos vemos en la estación a las 9
noss behmoss en la estath-yon a lass nweh-beh

can I have two tickets for tonight's performance?
quisiera dos entradas para esta noche
keesee-ehra doss entradass para esta nocheh

do you want to dance?
¿quieres bailar?
kee-ehress b'eye'-lar

do you want to dance again?
¿quieres bailar otra vez?
kee-ehress b'eye'-lar otra beth

thanks but I'm with my boyfriend
gracias, pero estoy con mi novio
grath-yass pairo estoy kon mee nob-yo

let's go out for some fresh air
vamos a tomar el aire
bamoss a tomar el a-aireh

will you let me back in again later?
¿puedo volver a entrar más tarde?
pwehdo bolbair a entrar mass tardeh

I'm meeting someone inside
he quedado con alguien dentro
eh kehdado kon alg-yen dentro

autorizada para mayores de 18 años	for adults only
cerrado	closed
en versión original	in the original language
intermedio	interval
localidades	tickets
sesión numerada	advance booking

THE BEACH

beach	la playa *pla-ya*
beach umbrella	una sombrilla *sombree-ya*
bikini	un bikini *beekeenee*
dive	tirarse de cabeza *teerarseh deh kabeh-tha*
sand	la arena *arehna*
sea	el mar *mar*
sunbathe	tomar el sol *tomar el sol*
suntan lotion	la leche bronceadora *lecheh brontheh-adora*
suntan oil	el aceite bronceador *athehteh brontheh-ador*
swim	nadar *nadar*
swimming costume	un bañador *ban-yador*
tan (*verb*)	ponerse moreno *ponairseh morehno*
towel	la toalla *to-a-ya*
wave	la ola *ola*

let's go down to the beach
vamos a la playa
bamoss a la pla-ya

what's the water like?
¿qué tal está el agua?
keh tal esta el agwa

it's freezing
está helada
esta ehlada

it's beautiful
es precioso
ess preth-yoso

are you coming for a swim?
¿vienes a bañarte?
b-yehness a ban-yarteh

THE BEACH

I can't swim
no sé nadar
no seh nadar

he swims like a fish
nada muy bien
nada mwee b-yen

will you keep an eye on my things for me?
¿puede cuidarme mis cosas?
pwehdeh kweedarmeh meess kossass

is it deep here?
¿cubre aquí?
koobreh akee

could you rub suntan oil on my back?
¿puedes ponerme crema en la espalda?
pwehdess ponairmeh krehma en la espalda

I love sun bathing
me encanta tomar el sol
meh enkanta tomar el sol

I'm all sunburnt
estoy todo quemado/a
estoy todo kehmado/a

you're all wet!
estás todo mojado/a
estass todo moнado/a

let's go up to the cafe
vamos a la cafetería
bamoss a la kafehtairee-a

bañero	lifeguard
duchas	showers
prohibido bañarse	no swimming
se alquilan sombrillas	parasols/ deck chairs/
tumbonas/pedales	pedalos for hire

41

PROBLEMS

accident	un accidente	*aktheedenteh*
ambulance	una ambulancia	*amboolanth-ya*
broken	roto	*roto*
doctor	un médico	*medeeko*
emergency	una emergencia	*ehmairнenth-ya*
fire	un incendio	*eenthend-yo*
fire brigade	los bomberos	*bombaiross*
ill	enfermo	*enfairmo*
injured	herido	*ehreedo*
late	tarde	*tardeh*
out of order	estropeado	*estropeh-ado*
police	la policía	*poleethee-a*

can you help me? I'm lost
¿podría ayudarme? me he perdido
podree-a a-yoodarmeh? meh eh pairdeedo

I've lost my passport
he perdido mi pasaporte
eh pairdeedo mee passaporteh

I've locked myself out of my room
he perdido la llave y no puedo entrar en mi habitación
eh pairdeedo la yabeh ee no pwehdo entrar en mee
abeetath-yon

my luggage hasn't arrived
mi equipaje no ha llegado
mee ekeepaнeh no a yehgado

I can't get it open
no puedo abrirlo
no pwehdo abreerlo

it's jammed
está atascado
esta ataskado

42

PROBLEMS

I don't have enough money
no tengo bastante dinero
no teng-go bastanteh deenehro

I've broken down
he tenido una avería
eh tehneedo oona abehree-a

can I use your telephone please, this is an emergency
¿puedo usar su teléfono? es una emergencia
pwehdo oossar soo teh-leh-fono ess oona ehmairнenth-ya

help!
¡socorro!
sokorro

it doesn't work
no funciona
no foonth-yona

the lights aren't working in my room
la luz no funciona en mi habitación
la looth no foonth-yona en mee abeetath-yon

the lift is stuck
el ascensor está atascado
el asthensor esta ataskado

I can't understand a single word
no entiendo nada
no ent-yendo nada

can you get an interpreter?
¿puede conseguir un intérprete?
pwehdeh konsegeer oon eentairprehteh

the toilet won't flush
la cisterna del water no funciona
la theestairna del vatair no foonth-yona

there's no plug in the bath
no hay tapón en la bañera
no 'eye' tapon en la ban-yehra

there's no hot water
no hay agua caliente
no 'eye' agwa kal-yenteh

43

PROBLEMS

there's no toilet paper left
no queda papel higiénico
no kehda papel ee-нee-eneeko

I'm afraid I've accidentally broken the ...
lo siento mucho, pero sin querer he roto el/ la ...
lo s-yento moocho pairo seen kehrair eh roto el/ la

this man has been following me
este hombre me ha estado siguiendo
esteh ombreh meh a estado seeg-yendo

I've been mugged
me han asaltado
meh an assaltado

my handbag has been stolen
me han robado el bolso
meh an robado la bolsa

bomberos	fire brigade
cuidado con el perro	beware of the dog
cuidado con ...	caution
desprendimiento de terreno	danger of landslides
no funciona	out of order
oficina de objetos perdidos	lost property office
peligro	danger
peligro de incendio	beware of starting fires
prohibido ...	no ...
rómpase en caso de emergencia	break in case of emergency
salida de emergencia	emergency exit

bandage	la venda *benda*
blood	la sangre *sangreh*
broken	roto *roto*
burn	la quemadura *kehmadoora*
chemist's	la farmacia *farmath-ya*
contraception	la anticoncepción *anteekonthepth-yon*
dentist	un dentista *denteesta*
disabled	minusválido *meenoosbaleedo*
disease	una enfermedad *enfairmehda*
doctor	un médico *medeeko*
health	la salud *saloo*
hospital	el hospital *ospeetal*
ill	enfermo *enfairmo*
nurse	una enfermera *enfairmehra*
wound	una herida *ehreeda*

I don't feel well
no me encuentro bien
no meh enkwentro b-yen

it's getting worse
está empeorando
esta empeh-orando

I feel better
me encuentro mejor
meh enkwentro meh-нor

I feel sick
estoy mareado
estoy mareh-ado

I've got a pain here
me duele aquí
meh dwehleh akee

it hurts
me duele
meh dwehleh

HEALTH

he's got a high temperature
tiene mucha fiebre
t-yeneh moocha f-yebreh

could you call a doctor?
¿podría llamar a un médico?
podree-a yamar a oon medeeko

is it serious?
¿es grave?
ess grabeh

will he need an operation?
¿necesitará una operación?
neth-ehseetara oona opeh-rath-yon

I'm diabetic
soy diabético
soy dee-abehteeko

keep her warm
¡que no coja frío!
keh no koнa free-o

have you got anything for ...?
¿tiene algo para ...?
t-yeneh algo para

agítese antes de usarse	shake before use
analgésico	painkiller
casa de socorro	first-aid post
con receta médica	sold on prescription
disuélvase	dissolve
médico	doctor's surgery
para uso externo	not to be taken internally
puesto de socorro	emergency medical service
somnífero	sleeping pill
tómese antes de las comidas	to be taken before meals
tómese ... veces al día	to be taken ... times a day
tranquilizante	tranquillizer

I want to learn to sailboard
quisiera aprender a practicar la tabla a vela
keesee-ehra aprendair a prakteekar la tabla a behla

can we hire a sailing boat?
¿podemos alquilar un barco de vela?
podehmoss alkeelar oon barko deh behla

how much is half an hour's waterskiing?
¿cuánto cuesta media hora de esquí acuático?
kwanto kwesta mehd-ya ora deh eskee akwateeko

I'd like lessons in skin-diving
quisiera unas lecciones de submarinismo
keesee-ehra oonass lekth-yoness deh soobmareeneesmo

can we use the tennis court?
¿podemos usar la pista de tenis?
podehmoss oossar la peesta deh teneess

I'd like to go and watch a local football match
quisiera ir a ver un partido de fútbol local
keesee-ehra eer a bair oon parteedo deh footbol lokal

is it possible to do any horse-riding here?
¿se puede montar a caballo aquí?
seh pwehdeh montar a kaba-yo akee

I'm here to play golf
he venido a jugar al golf
eh behneedo a Hoogar al golf

we're going to do some hill-walking
vamos a hacer montañismo
bamoss a athair montan-yeesmo

this is the first time I've ever tried it
es la primera vez que lo intento
ess la preemaira beth keh lo eentento

THE POST OFFICE

letter	la carta *karta*
poste restante	la lista de correos *leesta deh korreh-oss*
post office	correos *korreh-oss*
recorded delivery	con acuse de recibo *kon akoosseh deh reh-theebo*
send	enviar *enb-yar*
stamp	un sello *seh-yo*
telegram	un telegrama *teh-leh-grama*

how much is a letter to Ireland?
¿cuánto cuesta un sello para carta para Irlanda?
kwanto kwesta oon seh-yo para karta para eerlanda

I'd like four 30 peseta stamps
quisiera cuatro sellos de treinta pesetas
keesee-ehra kwatro seh-yoss deh trehnta pesehtass

I'd like six stamps for postcards to England
quisiera seis sellos para postales para Inglaterra
keesee-ehra sehss seh-yoss para postahless para eenglatehra

is there any mail for me?
¿hay alguna carta para mí?
'eye' algoona karta para mee

I'm expecting a parcel from ...
estoy esperando un paquete de ...
estoy espehrando oon pakehteh deh

código postal	post code
destinatario	addressee
horario de recogidas	collections
oficina de correos y telégrafos	post office and telegrams
remitente	sender
sellos	stamps

48

directory enquiries	la información *eenformath-yon*
engaged	comunicando *komooneekando*
extension	la extensión *ekstens-yon*
number	el número *noomehro*
operator	la operadora *opeh-radora*
phone (*verb*)	telefonear *teh-leh-foneh-ar*
phone box	una cabina telefónica *kabeena teh-leh-foneeka*
telephone	el teléfono *teh-leh-fono*
telephone directory	la guía de teléfonos *gee-a deh teh-leh-fonoss*

is there a phone round here?
¿hay un teléfono por aquí?
'eye' oon teh-leh-fono por akee

can I use your phone?
¿puedo usar su teléfono?
pwehdo oossar soo teh-leh-fono

I'd like to make a phone call to Britain
quisiera llamar a Gran Bretaña
keesee-ehra yamar a gran bretan-ya

I want to reverse the charges
quiero poner una conferencia a cobro revertido
kee-ehro ponair oona konfairenthee-a a kobro rehvairteedo

hello (*calling*)
hola
ola
(*answering*)
dígame
deegameh

could I speak to Patricia?
quisiera hablar con Patricia
keesee-ehra ablar kon Patricia

TELEPHONING

hello, this is Simon speaking
hola, soy Simon
ola soy Simon

can I leave a message?
¿podría dejar un recado?
podree-a deh-нar oon rehkahdo

do you speak English?
¿habla inglés?
abla eenglehss

could you say that again very very slowly?
¿puede repetir eso mucho más despacio?
pwehdeh rehpehteer esso moocho mass despath-yo

could you tell him Jim called?
¿podría decirle que ha llamado Jim?
podree-a deh-theerleh keh ah yamado Jim

could you ask her to ring me back?
¿podría decirle que me llame?
podree-a deh-theerleh keh meh yameh

I'll call back later
llamaré más tarde
yamareh mass tardeh

my number is . . .
mi número es . . .
mee noomehro ess

776-3211
siete siete seis tres dos uno uno
see-ehteh see-ehteh sehss tress doss oono oono

just a minute please
un momento por favor
oon momento por fabor

he's not in
no está
no esta

sorry, I've got the wrong number
lo siento, me he equivocado de número
lo s-yento meh eh ekeebokado deh noomehro

TELEPHONING

it's a terrible line
se oye muy mal
seh o-yeh mwee mal

REPLIES

no cuelgue
no kwel-geh
hang on

¿de parte de quién?
deh parteh deh kyen
who's calling?

cabina telefónica	telephone box
descuelgue el auricular	lift the receiver
guía telefónica	phone book
inserte moneda	insert coin
marcar el ...	dial ...
teléfono interurbano	long-distance phone

THE ALPHABET

how do you spell it?
¿cómo se escribe?
komo seh eskreebeh

I'll spell it
se lo deletreo
seh lo dehlehtreh-o

a *ah*	g *Heh*	m *emeh*	s *eseh*	x *ekiss*
b *beh*	h *acheh*	n *eneh*	t *teh*	y *ee gree-ehga*
c *theh*	i *ee*	o *o*	u *oo*	z *thehta*
d *deh*	j *Hota*	p *peh*	v *oobeh*	
e *eh*	k *ka*	q *koo*	w *oobeh*	
f *efeh*	l *eleh*	r *ereh*	*dobleh*	

NUMBERS, THE DATE, THE TIME

0	cero *thehro*
1	uno *oono*
2	dos *doss*
3	tres *tress*
4	cuatro *kwatro*
5	cinco *theenko*
6	seis *sehss*
7	siete *see-eh-teh*
8	ocho *ocho*
9	nueve *nweh-beh*
10	diez *dee-eth*
11	once *on-theh*
12	doce *dotheh*
13	trece *treh-theh*
14	catorce *katortheh*
15	quince *keentheh*
16	dieciséis *dee-eth-ee-sehss*
17	diecisiete *dee-eth-ee-see-eh-teh*
18	dieciocho *dee-eth-ee-ocho*
19	diecinueve *dee-eth-ee-nweh-beh*
20	veinte *behnteh*
21	veintiuno *behntee-oono*
22	veintidós *behntee-doss*
30	treinta *trehnta*
35	treinta y cinco *trehnt-ee-theenko*
40	cuarenta *kwarenta*
50	cincuenta *theenkwenta*
60	sesenta *sessenta*
70	setenta *setenta*
80	ochenta *ochenta*
90	noventa *nobenta*
100	cien *thee-en*

NUMBERS, THE DATE, THE TIME

101	ciento uno	*thee-ento oono*
200	doscientos	*doss-thee-entoss*
300	trescientos	*tress-thee-entoss*
400	cuatrocientos	*kwatro-thee-entoss*
500	quinientos	*keen-yentoss*
600	seiscientos	*sehss-thee-entoss*
700	setecientos	*seh-teh-thee-entoss*
800	ochocientos	*ocho-thee-entoss*
900	novecientos	*nobeh-thee-entoss*
1,000	mil	*meel*
2,000	dos mil	*doss meel*
5,000	cinco mil	*theenko meel*

what's the date?
¿qué fecha es hoy?
keh fecha ess oy

it's the 12th of January 1994
hoy es 12 de enero de 1994
*oy ess dotheh deh enehro deh meel nobeh-thee-entoss nobenta
ee kwatro*

what time is it?
¿qué hora es?
keh ora ess

it's midday/ midnight
es mediodía/ medianoche
ess mehd-yo-dee-a/ mehd-ya-nocheh

it's one/ three o'clock
es la una/ son las tres
ess la oona/ son lass tress

it's half past eight
son las ocho y media
son lass ocho ee mehd-ya

it's a quarter past/ to five
son las cinco y cuarto/ menos cuarto
son lass theenko ee kwarto/ menoss kwarto

it's six a.m./ p.m.
son las seis de la mañana/ la tarde
son lass sehss deh la man-yana/ la tardeh

at two/ five p.m.
a las dos/ cinco de la tarde
a lass doss/ theenko deh la tardeh

A

a un, *f* una
about (*approx*) aproximadamente
above encima de
abroad en el extranjero
accelerator el acelerador
accent el acento
accept aceptar
accident el accidente
accommodation el alojamiento
accompany acompañar
ache el dolor
adaptor el adaptador
address la dirección
address book la libreta de direcciones
adult el adulto
advance: in advance por adelantado
advise aconsejar
aeroplane el avión
afraid: I'm afraid (of) tengo miedo (de/ a)
after después (de)
afternoon la tarde
aftershave el after-shave
afterwards después
again otra vez
against contra
age la edad
agency la agencia
agent el representante
aggressive agresivo

ago: three days ago hace tres días
agree: I agree estoy de acuerdo
AIDS el SIDA
air el aire
air-conditioned con aire acondicionado
air-conditioning el aire acondicionado
air hostess la azafata
airline la compañía aérea
airmail: by airmail por avión
airport el aeropuerto
alarm la alarma
alarm clock el despertador
alcohol el alcohol
alive vivo
all: all men/ women todos los hombres/ todas las mujeres; **all the wine/ beer** todo el vino/ toda la cerveza; **all day** todo el día
allergic to alérgico a
all-inclusive todo incluido
allow permitir
allowed permitido
all right (*OK*) ¡bien!
almost casi
alone solo
already ya
also también
alternator el alternador
although aunque
altogether en total
always siempre
a.m.: at 5 a.m. a las 5 de la mañana

ambulance la ambulancia
America América f
American americano
among entre
amp: 15-amp de 15 amperios
ancestor el antepasado
anchor el ancla f
ancient antiguo
and y
angina la angina
angry enfadado
animal el animal
ankle el tobillo
anniversary (*wedding*) el aniversario de boda
annoying molesto
anorak el anorak
another otro
answer la respuesta
answer (*verb*) responder
ant la hormiga
antibiotic el antibiótico
antifreeze el anticongelante
antihistamine el antihistamínico
antique la antigüedad
antique shop la tienda de antigüedades
antiseptic el antiséptico
any: have you got any butter/ bananas? ¿tiene mantequilla/ plátanos?; **I don't have any** no tengo
anyway de todas formas
apartment el apartamento
aperitif el aperitivo
apologize disculparse
appalling terrible
appendicitis la apendicitis
appetite el apetito
apple la manzana
apple pie la tarta de manzana
appointment la cita

apricot el albaricoque
April abril
archaeology la arqueología
area la zona
arm el brazo
arrest detener
arrival la llegada
arrive llegar
art el arte
art gallery el museo de arte
artificial artificial
artist el/ la artista
as (*since*) como; **as beautiful as** tan bonito como
ashamed avergonzado
ashtray el cenicero
ask preguntar
asleep dormido
asparagus los espárragos
aspirin la aspirina
asthma el asma f
astonishing increíble
at: at the station en la estación; **at Betty's** en casa de Betty; **at 3 o'clock** a las tres
Atlantic el Atlántico
attractive atractivo
aubergine la berenjena
audience el público
August agosto
aunt la tía
Australia Australia f
Australian australiano
Austria Austria f
automatic automático
autumn el otoño
awake (*adjective*) despierto
awful horrible
axe el hacha f
axle el eje

B

baby el bebé
baby-sitter la cangura
bachelor el soltero
back la parte de atrás; *(of body)* la espalda; **back wheel/ seat** la rueda trasera/ el asiento trasero
backpack la mochila
bacon el bacon
bad malo
badly mal
bag la bolsa
bake cocer en el horno
baker's la panadería
balcony el balcón
bald calvo
ball la pelota
banana el plátano
bandage la venda
bank el banco
bar el bar
barbecue la barbacoa
barber el barbero
barmaid la camarera
barman el barman
basement el sótano
basket el cesto
bath el baño
bathing cap el gorro de baño
bathroom el cuarto de baño
bath salts las sales de baño
bathtub la bañera
battery la pila; *(for car)* la batería
be ser, estar *(see grammar)*
beach la playa
beans las judías; **green beans** judías verdes
beard la barba

beautiful bonito; *(person)* guapo
because porque
become hacerse
bed la cama; **single/ double bed** cama individual/ de matrimonio; **go to bed** acostarse
bed linen la ropa de cama
bedroom el dormitorio
bee la abeja
beef la carne de vaca
beer la cerveza
before antes; **before 5** antes de las cinco
begin empezar
beginner el/la principiante
beginning el principio
behind detrás (de)
beige beige
Belgian belga
Belgium Bélgica *f*
believe creer
bell la campana; *(for door)* el timbre
belong pertenecer
below debajo de
belt el cinturón
bend la curva
best: the best ... el/ la mejor ...
better mejor
between entre
bicycle la bicicleta
big grande
bikini el bikini
bill la cuenta
bird el pájaro
biro *(R)* el bolígrafo
birthday el cumpleaños; **happy birthday!** ¡feliz cumpleaños!
biscuit la galleta

bit: a little bit un poquito
bite la mordedura; (*insect*) la picadura
bitter amargo
black negro
black and white blanco y negro
blackberry la mora
bladder la vejiga
blanket la manta
bleach la lejía
bleed sangrar
bless you! ¡Jesús!
blind ciego
blister la ampolla
blocked obstruido
blond rubio
blood la sangre
blood group el grupo sanguíneo
blouse la blusa
blow-dry secar a mano
blue azul
boarding pass la tarjeta de embarque
boat el barco
body el cuerpo
boil hervir
bolt el cerrojo
bolt (*verb*) echar el cerrojo
bomb la bomba
bone el hueso
bonnet (*car*) el capó
book el libro
book (*verb*) reservar
bookshop la librería
boot (*shoe*) la bota; (*car*) el maletero
border la frontera
boring aburrido
born nacido; **I was born in 1963** nací en 1963
borrow pedir prestado

boss el jefe
both: both of them los dos
bottle la botella
bottle-opener el abrebotellas
bottom el fondo; (*of body*) el trasero; **at the bottom of** en el fondo de
bowl el cuenco
box la caja
box office la taquilla
boy el chico
boyfriend el novio
bra el sujetador
bracelet la pulsera
brake el freno
brake (*verb*) frenar
brandy el coñac
brave valiente
bread el pan; **white/ wholemeal bread** pan blanco/ integral
break romper
break down averiarse
breakdown (*car*) la avería; (*nervous*) la crisis nerviosa
breakfast el desayuno
breast el pecho
breastfeed amamantar
breathe respirar
brick el ladrillo
bridge (*over river*) el puente
briefcase la cartera
bring traer
Britain Gran Bretaña *f*
British británico
brochure el folleto
broke: I'm broke no tengo una perra
broken roto
brooch el broche
broom la escoba
brother el hermano
brother-in-law el cuñado

ENGLISH-SPANISH

brown marrón
bruise el cardenal
brush el cepillo
Brussels sprouts las coles de Bruselas
bucket el cubo
building el edificio
bulb (*light*) la bombilla
bull el toro
bullfight la corrida de toros
bumper el parachoques
bunk beds las literas
buoy la boya
burn la quemadura
burn (*verb*) quemar
bus el autobús
business el negocio
business trip el viaje de negocios
bus station la estación de autobuses
bus stop la parada del autobús
busy ocupado
but pero
butcher's la carnicería
butter la mantequilla
butterfly la mariposa
button el botón
buy comprar
by por; **by car** en coche

cabbage la col
cabin (*ship*) el camarote
cable car el teleférico
café la cafetería
cagoule el chubasquero
cake la tarta

cake shop la pastelería
calculator la calculadora
calendar el calendario
call llamar
calm down tranquilizarse
Calor gas (*R*) la bombona de gas
camera (*still*) la máquina de fotos; (*movie*) la cámara
campbed la cama de campaña
camping el camping
campsite el camping
can la lata
can: I/ he can puedo/ puede; **can you?** ¿puede?
Canada el Canadá
Canadian canadiense
cancel anular
candle la vela
canoe la piragua
cap la gorra
captain el capitán
car el coche
caravan la caravana
caravan site el camping
carburettor el carburador
card la tarjeta; (*playing*) la carta
cardboard el cartón
cardigan la chaqueta
car driver el/la automovilista
care: take care of ocuparse de
careful cuidadoso; **be careful!** ¡tenga cuidado!
car park el aparcamiento
carpet la alfombra
car rental el alquiler de coches
carriage el vagón
carrot la zanahoria
carry llevar
carry-cot el capazo

cash: pay cash pagar al contado
cash desk la caja
cash dispenser el cajero automático
cassette la cassette
cassette player el cassette
castle el castillo
cat el gato
catch coger
cathedral la catedral
Catholic católico
cauliflower la coliflor
cause la causa
cave la cueva
ceiling el techo
cemetery el cementerio
centigrade centígrado
central heating la calefacción central
centre el centro
century el siglo
certificate el certificado
chain la cadena
chair la silla
chairlift el telesilla
chambermaid la camarera
chance: by chance por casualidad
change el cambio
change cambiar; (*clothes*) cambiarse; **change trains** cambiar de tren
changeable (*weather*) variable
Channel el canal de la Mancha
charter flight el vuelo chárter
cheap barato
check (*verb*) revisar
check-in el mostrador de facturación
cheers! ¡salud!
cheese el queso

chemist's la farmacia
cheque el cheque
cheque book el talonario de cheques
cheque card la tarjeta de banco
cherry la cereza
chest el pecho
chestnut la castaña
chewing gum el chicle
chicken el pollo
child (*boy*) el niño; (*girl*) la niña
children's portion la ración pequeña para niños
chin la barbilla
chips las patatas fritas
chocolate el chocolate; **milk/ plain chocolate** chocolate con leche/ de hacer; **hot chocolate** chocolate caliente
choke el starter
choose elegir
chop (*meat*) la chuleta
Christian name el nombre de pila
Christmas Navidad *f*; **happy Christmas** Felices Navidades
church la iglesia
cider la sidra
cigar el puro
cigarette el cigarrillo
cigarette lighter el encendedor
cinema el cine
city la ciudad
city centre el centro de la ciudad
class la clase; **first/ second class** primera/ segunda clase
classical music la música

clásica

clean limpio

clean (*verb*) limpiar

cleansing cream la crema limpiadora

clear claro

clever listo

cliff el acantilado

climate el clima

cloakroom (*coats*) el guardarropa

clock el reloj

close (*verb*) cerrar

closed cerrado

clothes la ropa

clothes peg la pinza de la ropa

cloud la nube

cloudy nublado

club el club

clutch el embrague

coach el autobús

coast la costa

coat el abrigo

coathanger la percha

cockroach la cucaracha

cocktail el cóctel

cocoa el cacao

coffee el café; **white coffee** café con leche

cold frío; **it is cold** hace frío

cold (*illness*) el resfriado; **I've got a cold** tengo catarro

cold cream la crema de belleza

collar el cuello

collection la colección

colour el color

colour film la película en color

comb el peine

come venir; **I come from Madrid** soy de Madrid; **come back** volver; **come in!** ¡adelante!

comfortable cómodo

compact disc el disco compacto

company la compañía

compartment el compartimento

compass la brújula

complain quejarse

complicated complicado

compliment el cumplido

computer la computadora

concert el concierto

conditioner el acondicionador de pelo

condom el condón

conductor (*bus*) el cobrador

confirm confirmar

congratulations! ¡enhorabuena!

connection el enlace

constipated estreñido

consulate el consulado

contact (*verb*) ponerse en contacto con

contact lenses las lentillas

contraceptive el anticonceptivo

cook (*verb*) cocinar; (*boil*) cocer

cook el cocinero, la cocinera

cooker la cocina

cooking utensils los utensilios de cocina

cool fresco

corkscrew el sacacorchos

corner el rincón; (*of street*) la esquina

correct correcto

corridor el pasillo
cosmetics los cosméticos
cost costar
cot la cuna
cotton el algodón
cotton wool el algodón hidrófilo
couchette la litera
cough la tos
cough (*verb*) toser
country el país
countryside el campo
course: of course por supuesto
cousin el primo, la prima
cow la vaca
crab el cangrejo
crafts la artesanía
cramp el calambre
crankshaft el eje del cigüeñal
crash el accidente
crayfish la cigala
cream la nata
credit card la tarjeta de crédito
crew la tripulación
crisps las patatas fritas (en bolsa)
crockery la loza
cross (*verb*) cruzar
crowd la muchedumbre
crowded lleno
cruise el crucero
crutches las muletas
cry llorar
cucumber el pepino
cup la taza
cupboard el armario
curry el curry
curtain la cortina
custom la costumbre
customs la aduana
cut cortar

cutlery los cubiertos
cycling el ciclismo
cyclist el/la ciclista
cylinder head gasket la junta de culata

dad el papá
damage (*verb*) estropear
damp húmedo
dance (*verb*) bailar
danger el peligro
dangerous peligroso
dare atreverse
dark oscuro
dashboard el tablero de instrumentos
date (*time*) la fecha
daughter la hija
daughter-in-law la nuera
day el día; **the day before yesterday** anteayer; **the day after tomorrow** pasado mañana
dead muerto
deaf sordo
dear (*beloved*) querido
death la muerte
decaffeinated descafeinado
December diciembre
decide decidir
deck la cubierta
deck chair la tumbona
deep profundo
delay el retraso
deliberately a propósito
delicious delicioso
dentist el dentista
dentures la dentadura postiza

ENGLISH-SPANISH

deodorant el desodorante
department store los grandes almacenes
departure la salida
depend: it depends depende
depressed deprimido
dessert el postre
develop (*film*) revelar
device el aparato
diabetic diabético
dialect el dialecto
dialling code el prefijo
diamond el diamante
diarrhoea la diarrea
diary la agenda
dictionary el diccionario
die morir
diesel (*fuel*) el gas-oil
diet la dieta
different distinto
difficult difícil
dining car el coche-comedor
dining room el comedor
dinner la cena; **have dinner** cenar
direct directo
direction la dirección
directory enquiries la información
dirty sucio
disabled minusválido
disappear desaparecer
disappointed desilusionado
disaster el desastre
disco la discoteca
disease la enfermedad
disgusting repugnante
disinfectant el desinfectante
distance la distancia
distributor el distribuidor
district (*in town*) el barrio
disturb molestar
dive zambullirse; (*jump in*) tirarse al agua
divorced divorciado
do hacer
doctor el médico
document el documento
dog el perro
doll la muñeca
donkey el burro
door la puerta
double doble
double room la habitación doble
down abajo; **I feel a bit down** estoy triste
downstairs abajo
draught la corriente de aire
dream el sueño
dress el vestido
dress (*verb*) vestir; (*oneself*) vestirse
dressing gown la bata
drink la bebida
drink (*verb*) beber
drinking water el agua potable
drive conducir
driver el conductor
driving licence el permiso de conducir
drop la gota
drop (*verb*) dejar caer
drug (*narcotic*) la droga
drunk borracho
dry seco
dry (*verb*) secar
dry-cleaner la tintorería
duck el pato
durex (R) el preservativo
during durante
dustbin el cubo de la basura
Dutch holandés
duty-free shop la tienda libre de impuestos

E

each cada
ear la oreja
early temprano; (*too early*) demasiado pronto
earrings los pendientes
earth la tierra
east el este
Easter la Semana Santa
easy fácil
eat comer
eau de toilette el agua de colonia
egg el huevo; **boiled egg** huevo pasado por agua; **hard-boiled egg** huevo duro
egg cup la huevera
either ... or ... o ... o ...
elastic elástico
Elastoplast (R) la tirita
elbow el codo
electric eléctrico
electricity la electricidad
else: **something else** algo más
elsewhere en otra parte
embarrassing violento
embassy la embajada
emergency la emergencia
emergency exit la salida de emergencia
empty vacío
end el final
engaged (*toilet, phone*) ocupado; (*to be married*) prometido
engine el motor; (*train*) la locomotora
England Inglaterra *f*

English inglés
English girl/ woman la inglesa
Englishman el inglés
enlargement la ampliación
enough bastante
enter entrar (en)
entrance la entrada
envelope el sobre
epileptic epiléptico
especially especialmente
Eurocheque el eurocheque
Europe Europa *f*
European europeo
even: **even more beautiful** aún más bonito; **even men/ if** hasta los hombres/ incluso si
evening la tarde; **good evening** buenas tardes; (*later*) buenas noches
every cada
everyone todos
everything todo
everywhere por todas partes
exaggerate exagerar
example el ejemplo; **for example** por ejemplo
excellent excelente
except excepto
excess baggage el exceso de equipaje
exchange (*verb*) cambiar
exchange rate el tipo de cambio
exciting emocionante
excuse me perdone
exhaust el tubo de escape
exhibition la exposición
exit la salida
expensive caro
explain explicar
extension lead el cable

alargador
eye el ojo
eyebrow la ceja
eyeliner el lápiz de ojos
eye shadow la sombra de ojos

F

face la cara
factory la fábrica
faint (*verb*) desmayarse
fair (*funfair*) las ferias
fair (*adjective*) justo
fall caerse
false falso
family la familia
famous famoso
fan el ventilador
fan belt la correa del ventilador
far away lejos
farm la granja
farmer el agricultor
fashion la moda
fashionable de moda
fast rápido
fat la grasa
fat (*adjective*) gordo
father el padre
father-in-law el suegro
fault: it's my/ his fault es culpa mía/ suya
faulty defectuoso
favourite favorito
fear el miedo
February febrero
fed up: I'm fed up (with) estoy harto (de)

feel sentir; **I feel well/ unwell** me/ no me siento bien; **I feel like ...** me apetece ...
feeling el sentimiento
felt-tip pen el rotulador
feminist feminista
fence la valla
ferry el ferry
fever la fiebre
few: few tourists pocos turistas; **a few tourists** algunos turistas
fiancé, fiancée el novio, la novia
field el campo
fight la pelea
fight (*verb*) pelear
fill llenar
fillet el filete
filling (*tooth*) el empaste
film la película
filter el filtro
find encontrar
fine la multa
fine (*good*) bueno
finger el dedo
fingernail la uña
finish terminar
fire el fuego
fire brigade los bomberos
fire extinguisher el extintor
fireworks los fuegos artificiales
first primero
first aid los primeros auxilios
first class la primera (clase)
first floor el primer piso
first name el nombre de pila
fish el pez; (*to eat*) el pescado
fishbone la espina
fishing la pesca

fishmonger's la pescadería
fit (*healthy*) en forma
fizzy con gas
flag la bandera
flash el flash
flat el piso
flat (*adjective*) plano; (*tyre*) pinchado
flavour el sabor
flea la pulga
flight el vuelo
flirt coquetear
floor (*of room*) el suelo; (*storey*) el piso
florist's la floristería
flour la harina
flower la flor
flu la gripe
fly la mosca
fly (*verb*) volar
fog la niebla
folk music la música folklórica
follow seguir
food la comida
food poisoning la intoxicación alimenticia
foot, el pie; **on foot** a pie
football el fútbol
for para; (*because of*) por; (*during*) durante
forbidden prohibido
forehead la frente
foreign extranjero
foreigner el extranjero
forest el bosque
forget olvidar
fork el tenedor; (*in road*) la bifurcación
form (*to fill in*) el impreso
fortnight quince días
fortunately afortunadamente

forward (*mail*) remitir
foundation cream la crema base
fountain la fuente
fracture la fractura
France Francia
free libre; (*of charge*) gratis
freezer el congelador
French francés
fresh fresco
Friday viernes
fridge el frigorífico
friend el amigo, la amiga
from de
front la parte delantera; **in front of** delante de
frost la escarcha
frozen (*food*) congelado
fruit la fruta
fry freír
frying pan la sartén
full lleno
full board la pensión completa
fun: have fun divertirse
funeral el funeral
funnel (*for pouring*) el embudo
funny (*amusing*) gracioso; (*strange*) raro
furious furioso
furniture los muebles
further más allá
fuse el fusible
future el futuro

game (*to play*) el juego; (*meat*) la caza

garage el garaje
garden el jardín
garlic el ajo
gas el gas
gas permeable lenses las lentillas porosas
gauge el indicador de nivel
gay homosexual
gear la velocidad
gearbox la caja de cambios
gear lever la palanca de velocidades
gentleman el señor
gents (*toilet*) los servicios de caballeros
genuine auténtico
German alemán
Germany Alemania *f*
get obtener; (*for someone*) traer; **how do I get to ...?** ¿podría decirme cómo llegar a ...?
get across cruzar
get back (*return*) volver
get in (*car*) subir
get off bajarse
get out! ¡váyase!
get up levantarse
gin la ginebra
gin and tonic la tónica con ginebra
girl la chica
girlfriend la novia
give dar
give back devolver
glad alegre
glass el cristal; (*drinking*) el vaso
glasses las gafas
gloves los guantes
glue el pegamento
go ir; **go away!** ¡váyase!
go down bajar

go in entrar
go out salir
go through pasar por
go up subir
goat la cabra
God Dios *m*
gold el oro
golf el golf
good bueno; **good!** ¡bien!
goodbye adiós
goose el ganso
got: have you got ...? ¿tiene ...?
government el gobierno
grammar la gramática
grandfather el abuelo
grandmother la abuela
grapefruit el pomelo
grapes las uvas
grass la hierba
grateful agradecido
greasy grasiento
Greece Grecia *f*
Greek griego
green verde
greengrocer la frutería
grey gris
grilled a la parrilla
grocer's la tienda de comestibles
ground floor la planta baja
group el grupo
guarantee la garantía
guest el invitado
guesthouse la casa de huéspedes
guide el guía
guidebook la guía
guitar la guitarra
gun (*rifle*) la escopeta

H

habit la costumbre
hail el granizo
hair el pelo
haircut el corte de pelo
hairdresser's la peluquería
hair dryer el secador de pelo
hair spray la laca
half la mitad; **half a litre/ bottle** medio litro/ media botella; **half an hour** media hora
half board la media pensión
ham el jamón
hamburger la hamburguesa
hammer el martillo
hand la mano
handbag el bolso
handbrake el freno de mano
handkerchief el pañuelo
handle (of door) el picaporte; (of suitcase) el asa
hand luggage el equipaje de mano
handsome guapo
hanger la percha
hangover la resaca
happen suceder
happy contento
harbour el puerto
hard duro
hard lenses las lentillas duras
hat el sombrero
hate odiar
have tener (see grammar); **I/ you have to ...** tengo/ tiene que ...
hay fever la fiebre del heno
hazelnut la avellana

he él (see grammar)
head la cabeza
headache el dolor de cabeza
headlights los faros
health la salud
healthy sano
hear oír
hearing aid el audífono
heart el corazón
heart attack el ataque al corazón
heat el calor
heater (in room) el calentador
heating la calefacción
heavy pesado
heel el talón
helicopter el helicóptero
hello ¡hola!
help la ayuda; **help!** ¡socorro!
help (verb) ayudar
her (possessive) su; (pronoun) la, ella, le (see grammar)
herbs las hierbas
here aquí; **here is/are** aquí está/están
hers suyo (see grammar)
hiccups el hipo
hide (something) esconder
high alto
highway code el código de la circulación
hill la colina
him le, él (see grammar)
hip la cadera
hire: for hire se alquila
his su; **it's his** es suyo (see grammar)
history la historia
hit golpear
hitchhike hacer autostop
hitchhiking el autostop
hobby el pasatiempo

hold tener
hole el agujero
holiday las vacaciones;
(*public*) la fiesta; **the
summer holidays** las
vacaciones de verano
Holland Holanda *f*
home: at home en casa; go
home volver a casa
homemade de fabricación
casera
homesick: I'm homesick
tengo morriña
honest honrado
honey la miel
honeymoon el viaje de
novios
hoover (*R*) la aspiradora
hope (*verb*) esperar
horn la bocina
horrible horrible
horse el caballo
horse riding la equitación
hospital el hospital
hospitality la hospitalidad
hot caliente; (*to taste*)
picante
hotel el hotel
hot-water bottle la bolsa de
agua caliente
hour la hora
house la casa
house wine el vino de la casa
how? ¿cómo?
how many? ¿cuántos?
how much? ¿cuánto?
humour el humor
hungry: I'm hungry tengo
hambre
hurry darse prisa; hurry up!
¡dese prisa!
hurt doler
husband el marido

I yo
ice el hielo
ice cream el helado
ice lolly el polo
idea la idea
idiot el/la idiota
if si
ignition el encendido
ill enfermo
immediately
inmediatamente
important importante
impossible imposible
improve mejorar
in en; is he in? ¿está?
included incluido
incredible increíble
independent independiente
indicator (*of car*) el indicador
indigestion la indigestión
industry la industria
infection la infección
information la información
information desk la
información
injection la inyección
injured herido
inner tube la cámara
innocent inocente
insect el insecto
insect repellent la loción
contra insectos
inside adentro; inside the
house dentro de la casa
insomnia el insomnio
instant coffee el café
·instantáneo
instructor el instructor

ENGLISH-SPANISH

insurance el seguro
intelligent inteligente
interesting interesante
introduce presentar
invitation la invitación
invite invitar
Ireland Irlanda *f*
Irish irlandés
iron (*metal*) el hierro; (*for clothes*) la plancha
iron (*verb*) planchar
ironmonger's la ferretería
island la isla
it lo; **it is ...** (*see grammar*)
Italian italiano
Italy Italia *f*
itch el picor
IUD el DIU

jack (*car*) el gato
jacket la chaqueta
jam la mermelada
January enero
jaw la mandíbula
jazz el jazz
jealous celoso
jeans los vaqueros
jellyfish la medusa
jeweller's la joyería
jewellery las joyas
Jewish judío
job el trabajo
jogging: I go jogging hago footing
joint (*to smoke*) el porro
joke el chiste
journey el viaje; **have a good journey!** ¡buen viaje!

jug la jarra
juice el zumo
July julio
jump saltar
jumper el jersey
junction el cruce
June junio
just: just two sólo dos

keep quedarse
key la llave
kidney el riñón
kill matar
kilo el kilo
kilometre el kilómetro
kind amable
king el rey
kiss el beso
kiss (*verb*) besar
kitchen la cocina
knee la rodilla
knife el cuchillo
knit hacer punto
knock over (*car*) atropellar
know saber; (*person*) conocer; **I don't know** no sé

label la etiqueta
ladder la escalera
ladies (*toilet*) los aseos de señoras
lady la señora

lager la cerveza
lake el lago
lamb el cordero
lamp la lámpara
land (*verb*) aterrizar
landscape el paisaje
language el idioma
language school la escuela de idiomas
large grande
last último; **last year** el año pasado; **at last** por fin
late tarde; **it's late** (*bus etc*) tiene retraso; **later** más tarde
laugh reír
launderette la lavandería automática
laundry la ropa sucia
law la ley
lawn el césped
lawyer el abogado
laxative el laxante
lazy perezoso
leaf la hoja
leaflet el folleto
leak el escape
learn aprender
least: at least por lo menos
leather el cuero
leave (*go away*) irse; (*behind*) dejar; (*forget*) olvidar
left (*side*) la izquierda; **on the left (of)** a la izquierda (de)
left-handed zurdo
left luggage la consigna
leg la pierna
lemon el limón
lemonade la limonada
lend prestar
length la longitud
lens el objetivo
less menos

lesson la clase
let (*allow*) dejar
letter la carta
letterbox el buzón
lettuce la lechuga
level crossing el paso a nivel
library la biblioteca
licence el permiso
lid la tapa
lie (*say untruth*) mentir
lie down echarse
life la vida
lift levantar
lift (*elevator*) el ascensor; **give a lift** llevar en el coche
light (*in room*) la luz; (*on car*) el faro; **have you got a light?** ¿tiene fuego?
light (*adjective*) ligero; **light blue** azul claro
light (*verb*) encender
light bulb la bombilla
lighter el encendedor
lighthouse el faro
light meter el fotómetro
like: I like cheese/ sleeping me gusta el queso/ dormir; **I would like** quisiera
like (*as*) como
lip el labio
lipstick la barra de labios
liqueur el licor
list la lista
listen (to) escuchar
litre el litro
litter la basura
little pequeño; **a little bit of** un poco de
live vivir
liver el hígado
living room el cuarto de estar
lizard la lagartija
lobster la langosta

lock la cerradura
lock (verb) cerrar con llave
lollipop el chupa-chups
London Londres
long largo; **a long time**
mucho tiempo
look (at) mirar; (seem)
parecer
look for buscar
look like parecerse a
look out! ¡cuidado!
lorry el camión
lose perder
lost property office la oficina
de objetos perdidos
lot: **a lot of wine/ cars** mucho
vino/ muchos coches
loud fuerte
lounge el cuarto de estar
love el amor; **make love**
hacer el amor
love (verb) querer
lovely encantador
low bajo
luck la suerte; **good luck!**
¡buena suerte!
luggage el equipaje
lukewarm tibio
lunch el almuerzo; (at home)
la comida
lungs los pulmones

macho varonil
mad loco
Madam señora
magazine la revista
maiden name el nombre de
soltera

mail el correo
main principal
make (verb) hacer
make-up el maquillaje
male chauvinist pig el
machista
man el hombre
manager el gerente
many: **many people/**
countries mucha gente/
muchos países
map el mapa; (of town) el
plano
March marzo
margarine la margarina
market el mercado
marmalade la mermelada de
naranja
married casado
mascara el rímel
mass la misa
match (for fire) la cerilla;
(sport) el partido
material la tela
matter: **it doesn't matter** no
importa
mattress el colchón
May mayo
maybe quizás
mayonnaise la mayonesa
me yo, me (see grammar)
meal la comida; **enjoy your**
meal! ¡buen provecho!
mean (verb) significar
measles el sarampión;
German measles la rubéola
meat la carne
mechanic el mecánico
medicine la medicina
medieval medieval
Mediterranean el
Mediterráneo
medium-sized de tamaño

medio
meet (*someone*) encontrar
meeting la reunión
melon el melón
mend arreglar
menu la carta; **set menu** el menú del día
mess el lío
message el recado
metal el metal
metre el metro
midday el mediodía
middle el medio
middle ages la edad media
midnight la media noche
milk la leche
minced meat la carne picada
mind: do you mind if I ...? ¿le importa si ...?
mine mío (*see grammar*)
mineral water el agua mineral
minute el minuto
mirror el espejo
Miss Señorita
miss (*train etc*) perder; **I miss you** te echo de menos
mistake el error
misunderstanding el malentendido
mix mezclar
modern moderno
moisturizer la crema hidratante
Monday lunes
money el dinero
month el mes
monument el monumento
mood el humor
moon la luna
more más; **more than** más que; **no more** ya no más
morning la mañana; **good**

morning buenos días
mosquito el mosquito
most of la mayor parte de
mother la madre
motorbike la moto
motorboat la motora
motorway la autopista
mountain la montaña
mouse el ratón
moustache el bigote
mouth la boca
move mover
Mr Señor
Mrs Señora
Ms Señora, Señorita
much mucho
mum la mamá
muscle el músculo
museum el museo
mushrooms los champiñones
music la música
musical instrument el instrumento musical
mussels los mejillones
must: I/ she must ... tengo/ tiene que ...
mustard la mostaza
my mi (*see grammar*)

N

nail (*in wall*) el clavo
nail clippers el cortauñas
nailfile la lima de uñas
nail polish el esmalte de uñas
nail polish remover el quitaesmalte
naked desnudo
name el nombre; **my name is Jim** me llamo Jim

napkin la servilleta
nappy el pañal
nappy-liners los salvapañales
narrow estrecho
nationality la nacionalidad
natural natural
nature la naturaleza
near cerca; **near here** cerca de aquí; **nearest** más cercano
nearly casi
necessary necesario
neck el cuello
necklace el collar
need: I need ... necesito ...
needle la aguja
negative (*film*) el negativo
neighbour el vecino, la vecina
neither ... nor ... ni ... ni ...
nephew el sobrino
nervous nervioso
neurotic neurótico
never nunca
new nuevo
news las noticias
newsagent el kiosko de periódicos
newspaper el periódico
New Year el Año Nuevo; **happy New Year** Feliz Año Nuevo
next próximo; (*following*) siguiente; **next year** el próximo año; **next to** al lado de
nice (*person*) simpático; (*meal*) bueno; (*place etc*) bonito
nickname el apodo
niece la sobrina
night la noche; **good night** buenas noches
nightclub el cabaret
nightdress el camisón
nightmare la pesadilla
no (*reply*) no; **there is no water** no hay agua; **there is no more sugar** no hay más azucar; **no longer** ya no más
nobody nadie
noise el ruido
noisy ruidoso
non-smoking no fumadores
normal normal
north el norte; **north of the town** al norte de la ciudad
Northern Ireland Irlanda del Norte *f*
nose la nariz
not no; **I'm not tired** no estoy cansado
notebook el cuaderno
nothing nada
novel la novela
November noviembre
now ahora
nowhere en ningún sitio
number (*house, phone*) el número
number plate la matrícula
nurse la enfermera
nut (*to eat*) la nuez; (*for bolt*) la tuerca

obnoxious desagradable
obvious evidente
October octubre
octopus el pulpo

of de (*see grammar*)
off (*light*) apagado
offend ofender
offer (*verb*) ofrecer
office la oficina
often a menudo
oil el aceite
ointment la pomada
OK vale; **I'm OK** estoy bien
old viejo; **I'm 25 years old** tengo 25 años
old-age pensioner el pensionista
olive la aceituna
olive oil el aceite de oliva
omelette la tortilla
on en; (*light*) encendido; **a book on** un libro sobre; **on Monday** el lunes
once una vez
one uno, una
onion la cebolla
only sólo
open abierto
open (*verb*) abrir
opera la ópera
operation la operación
opposite enfrente de
optician el óptico
optimistic optimista
or o
orange (*fruit*) la naranja
orange (*colour*) naranja
ours nuestro (*see grammar*)
out; he's out no está
orchestra la orquesta
order (*meal*) pedir
organize organizar
other otro
otherwise si no
our, ours nuestro (*see grammar*)
out: he's out no está

outside fuera
oven el horno
over (*above*) encima de; **over there** por allí
overdone muy hecho
overtake adelantar
owner el propietario
oyster la ostra

pack (*luggage*) hacer las maletas
package el paquete
package tour el viaje organizado
packed lunch la bolsa con la comida
packet el paquete
page la página
pain el dolor
painful doloroso
painkiller el analgésico
paint (*verb*) pintar
paint brush (*artist's*) el pincel
painting el cuadro
pair el par
palace el palacio
pancake la crêpe
panic el pánico
panties las bragas
paper el papel
parcel el paquete
pardon ? ¿cómo dice?
parents los padres
park (*garden*) el parque
park (*verb*) aparcar
part la parte
party (*celebration*) la fiesta; (*group*) el grupo

pass (*mountain*) el puerto
passenger el pasajero
passport el pasaporte
pasta la pasta
pâté el paté
path el camino
pavement la acera
pay pagar
peach el melocotón
peanuts los cacahuetes
pear la pera
peas los guisantes
pedal el pedal
pedestrian el peatón
pedestrian crossing el paso de peatones
pedestrian precinct la zona reservada para peatones
pen la pluma
pencil el lápiz
pencil sharpener el sacapuntas
penicillin la penicilina
penis el pene
penknife la navaja
people la gente
pepper (*spice*) la pimienta; (*vegetable*) el pimiento
per: per week por semana
per cent por ciento
perfect perfecto
perfume el perfume
period el período
perm la permanente
person la persona
petrol la gasolina
petrol station la gasolinera
phone (*verb*) telefonear; (*someone*) llamar por teléfono
phone book la guía telefónica
phone box la cabina telefónica

phone number el número de teléfono
photograph la fotografía
photograph (*verb*) fotografiar
photographer el fotógrafo
phrase book el libro de frases
pickpocket el carterista
picnic la merienda
pie (*fruit*) la tarta
piece el pedazo
pig el cerdo
piles las hemorroides
pill la píldora
pillow la almohada
pilot el piloto
pin el alfiler
pineapple la piña
pink rosa
pipe (*tube*) la tubería; (*to smoke*) la pipa
pity: it's a pity es una lástima
pizza la pizza
plane el avión
plant la planta
plastic el plástico; **plastic bag** la bolsa de plástico
plate el plato
platform el andén
play (*verb*) jugar
play (*in theatre*) la obra de teatro
pleasant agradable
please por favor
pleased contento; **pleased to meet you** mucho gusto
pliers los alicates
plug (*electrical*) el enchufe; (*in sink*) el tapón
plum la ciruela
plumber el fontanero
p.m.: at 3 p.m. a las 3 de la tarde
pneumonia la pulmonía

pocket el bolsillo
poison el veneno
police la policía
policeman el policía
police station la comisaría
polite educado
politics la política
polluted contaminado
pond el estanque
pony el poney
poor pobre
pop music la música pop
pork la carne de cerdo
port (*drink*) el Oporto;
    (*boats*) el puerto
porter (*hotel*) el conserje
Portugal Portugal *m*
Portuguese portugués
possible posible
post (*verb*) echar al buzón
postcard la postal
poster (*for room*) el poster; (*in street*) el cartel
poste restante la lista de
    Correos
postman el cartero
post office la oficina de
    Correos
potato la patata
poultry las aves
pound la libra
power cut el apagón
practical práctico
pram el cochecito
prawn la gamba
prefer preferir
pregnant embarazada
prepare preparar
prescription la receta
present (*gift*) el regalo
pretty bonito
price el precio
priest el cura

prince el príncipe
princess la princesa
printed matter el impreso
prison la cárcel
private privado
probably probablemente
problem el problema
programme el programa
prohibited prohibido
promise (*verb*) prometer
pronounce pronunciar
protect proteger
Protestant protestante
proud orgulloso
public público
pull tirar
pump la bomba
puncture el pinchazo
punk (*adjective*) punk
purple morado
purse el monedero
push empujar
pushchair la sillita de ruedas
put poner
pyjamas el pijama

quality la calidad
quarter el cuarto
quay el muelle
queen la reina
question la pregunta
queue la cola
queue (*verb*) hacer cola
quick rápido
quickly rápidamente
quiet tranquilo; **quiet!**
    ¡silencio!
quilt el edredón
quite bastante

R

rabbit el conejo
radiator el radiador
radio la radio
railway el ferrocarril
rain la lluvia
rain (*verb*) llover; **it's raining** está lloviendo
rainbow el arco iris
raincoat la gabardina
rape la violación
rare raro; (*steak*) poco pasado
raspberry la frambuesa
rat la rata
rather bastante
raw crudo
razor la máquina de afeitar
razor blade la cuchilla de afeitar
read leer
ready listo
really realmente
rear lights las luces traseras
rearview mirror el retrovisor
receipt el recibo
receive recibir
reception (*hotel*) la recepción
receptionist el/la recepcionista
recipe la receta
recognize reconocer
recommend recomendar
record el disco
record player el tocadiscos
record shop la tienda de discos
red rojo
red-headed pelirrojo

refund (*verb*) reembolsar
relax relajarse
religion la religión
remember recordar; **I remember** recuerdo
rent el alquiler
rent (*verb*) alquilar
repair reparar
repeat repetir
reservation la reserva
reserve reservar
responsible responsable
rest (*remaining*) el resto; **take a rest** descansar
restaurant el restaurante
return ticket el billete de ida y vuelta
reverse (*gear*) la marcha atrás
reverse charge call la llamada a cobro revertido
rheumatism el reumatismo
rib la costilla
rice el arroz
rich rico; (*food*) fuerte
ridiculous ridículo
right (*correct*) correcto
right (*side*) la derecha; **on the right (of)** a la derecha (de)
right of way la preferencia
ring (*on finger*) el anillo
ring (*phone*) llamar por teléfono
ripe maduro
river el río
road la carretera
roadsign la señal de tráfico
roadworks las obras
rock la roca
rock climbing la escalada
rock music el rock
roll el bollo
roof el tejado
roof rack la baca

room la habitación
rope la cuerda
rose la rosa
rosé wine el vino rosado
rotten podrido
round (*circular*) redondo
route la ruta
rowing boat la barca de remos
rubber la goma
rubber band la goma elástica
rubbish la basura
rucksack la mochila
rude grosero
rug la alfombra
ruins las ruinas
rum el ron
run correr

sad triste
safe seguro; (*out of danger*) fuera de peligro
safety pin el imperdible
sailboard la tabla a vela
sailing la vela
sailing boat el barco de vela
salad la ensalada
salad dressing el aliño para la ensalada
sale la venta; (*reduced prices*) las rebajas; **for sale** se vende
salmon el salmón
salt la sal
salty salado
same mismo
sand la arena
sandals las sandalias

sand dunes las dunas
sandwich el bocadillo
sanitary towel la compresa
sardine la sardina
Saturday sábado
sauce la salsa
saucepan el cazo
saucer el platillo
sauna la sauna
sausage la salchicha
savoury salado
say decir
scarf (*neck*) la bufanda; (*head*) el pañuelo
scenery el paisaje
school la escuela
science la ciencia
scissors las tijeras
Scotland Escocia *f*
Scottish escocés
scrambled eggs los huevos revueltos
scream gritar
screw el tornillo
screwdriver el destornillador
sea el mar
seafood los mariscos
seagull la gaviota
seasick: I'm seasick estoy mareado
seaside: at the seaside a la orilla del mar
season la temporada; **in the high season** en la temporada alta
seat el asiento
seat belt el cinturón de seguridad
seaweed las algas
second el segundo
second-hand de segunda mano
secret secreto

see ver; **see you tomorrow** hasta mañana
self-service el autoservicio
sell vender
sellotape (R) el papel celo
send enviar
sensible razonable
sensitive sensible
separate separado
separately por separado
September septiembre
serious serio
serve (meal) servir
service el servicio
service charge el servicio
serviette la servilleta
several varios
sew coser
sex (activity) el amor
sexist machista
sexy sexy
shade la sombra
shampoo el champú
share (verb) compartir
shark el tiburón
shave afeitarse
shaving brush la brocha de afeitar
shaving foam la espuma de afeitar
she ella (see grammar)
sheet la sábana
shell la concha
shellfish los mariscos
ship el barco
shirt la camisa
shock el susto
shock-absorber el amortiguador
shocking escandaloso
shoe laces los cordones de los zapatos
shoe polish el betún

shoe repairer el zapatero
shoes los zapatos
shop la tienda
shopping las compras; **go shopping** ir de compras
shopping bag la bolsa de la compra
shopping centre el centro comercial
shore la orilla
short corto
shortcut el atajo
shorts los pantalones cortos
shortsighted miope
shoulder el hombro
shout gritar
show (verb) mostrar
shower la ducha; (rain) el chaparrón
shutter (photo) el obturador
shutters (window) las contraventanas
shy tímido
sick: I feel sick estoy mareado; **I'm going to be sick** voy a devolver
side el lado
sidelights las luces de posición
sign (verb) firmar
silence el silencio
silk la seda
silver la plata
silver foil el papel de plata
similar parecido
simple sencillo
since (time) desde (que)
sincere sincero
sing cantar
single (unmarried) soltero
single room la habitación individual
single ticket el billete de ida

sink el fregadero
sink (*go under*) hundirse
sir señor
sister la hermana
sister-in-law la cuñada
sit down sentarse
size la talla
ski el esquí
ski (*verb*) esquiar
ski boots las botas de esquí
skid patinar
skiing el esquí
ski-lift el telesquí
skin la piel
skin cleanser la leche
  limpiadora
skin-diving el buceo
skinny flaco
skirt la falda
ski slope la pista de esquí
skull el cráneo
sky el cielo
sleep dormir
sleeper el coche-cama
sleeping bag el saco de
  dormir
sleeping pill el somnífero
sleepy: I'm sleepy tengo
  sueño
slice la rebanada
slide (*photo*) la diapositiva
slim delgado
slippers las zapatillas
slippery resbaladizo
slow lento
slowly despacio
small pequeño
smell el olor
smell (*verb*) oler
smile (*verb*) sonreír
smoke el humo
smoke (*verb*) fumar
smoking (*compartment*)

fumadores
snack un bocadillo
snake la culebra
sneeze estornudar
snore roncar
snow la nieve
so: so beautiful tan bonito; I
  hope so espero que sí; so
  do/am I yo también
soap el jabón
society la sociedad
socket el enchufe
socks los calcetines
soft suave
soft drink el refresco
soft lenses las lentillas
  blandas
sole (*of shoe*) la suela
some alguno; some
  wine/biscuits vino/ galletas
somebody alguien
something algo
sometimes a veces
somewhere en alguna parte
son el hijo
song la canción
son-in-law el yerno
soon pronto
sore: I've got a sore throat
  tengo dolor de garganta
sorry perdone
soup la sopa
sour ácido
south el sur; south of the
  town al sur de la ciudad
  ciudad
souvenir el recuerdo
space el espacio
spade la pala
Spain España *f*
Spanish español
spanner la llave inglesa
spare parts los repuestos

spare tyre la rueda de repuesto
spark plug la bujía
speak hablar
speciality la especialidad
speed la velocidad
speed limit el límite de velocidad
speedometer el velocímetro
spend gastar
spice la especia
spider la araña
spinach las espinacas
spoke (*bike*) el radio
spoon la cuchara
sport el deporte
spot (*on skin*) el grano
sprain: I've sprained my ankle me he torcido el tobillo
spring (*season*) la primavera; (*in seat etc*) el muelle
square (*in town*) la plaza
stain la mancha
stairs las escaleras
stamp el sello
stand: I can't stand cheese no aguanto el queso
star la estrella
starter (*food*) el entremés
state el estado
station la estación
stationer's la papelería
stay (*remain*) quedarse; (*in hotel etc*) hospedarse
stay (*noun*) la estancia
steak el filete
steal robar
steamer el vapor
steep empinado
steering la dirección
steering wheel el volante

stepfather el padrasto
stepmother la madrasta
steward el aeromozo
stewardess la azafata
still (*adverb*) todavía
sting picar
stockings las medias
stomach el estómago
stomach ache el dolor de estómago
stone la piedra
stop (*verb*) parar; **stop!** ¡deje!; (*car*) ¡pare!
stop la parada
storm la tormenta
story la historia
straight ahead todo derecho
strange (*odd*) extraño
strawberry la fresa
stream el arroyo
street la calle
string la cuerda
stroke (*attack*) la apoplejía
strong fuerte
stuck atascado
student el/ la estudiante
stupid estúpido
suburbs las afueras
success el éxito
suddenly de repente
suede el ante
sugar el azúcar
suit: blue suits you te sienta bien el azul
suit (*to wear*) el traje
suitcase la maleta
summer el verano
sun el sol
sunbathe tomar el sol
sunburn la quemadura de sol
Sunday domingo

ENGLISH-SPANISH

sunglasses las gafas de sol
sunny soleado
sunset la puesta de sol
sunshine la luz del sol
sunstroke la insolación
suntan el bronceado
suntan lotion la loción bronceadora
suntan oil el aceite bronceador
supermarket el supermercado
supplement el suplemento
sure seguro
surf el surf
surname el apellido
surprise la sorpresa
surprising sorprendente
swallow tragar
sweat sudar
sweater el suéter
sweet el caramelo
sweet dulce
swim nadar
swimming la natación; **go swimming** bañarse
swimming costume el traje de baño
swimming pool la piscina
swimming trunks el traje de baño
Swiss suizo
switch el interruptor
switch off (*light*) apagar; (*engine*) parar
switch on encender
Switzerland Suiza *f*
swollen inflamado
synagogue la sinagoga

table la mesa
tablecloth el mantel
tablet la pastilla
table tennis el ping-pong
tail la cola
take tomar
take away (*remove*) llevarse; **to take away** (*food*) para llevar
take off quitar; (*plane*) despegar
talcum powder el talco
talk hablar
tall alto
tampon el tampón
tan el bronceado
tank el depósito
tap el grifo
tape (*cassette*) la cinta
tart la tarta
taste el sabor
taste (*try*) probar
taxi el taxi
tea el té
teach enseñar
teacher el profesor, la profesora
team el equipo
teapot la tetera
tea towel el paño de cocina
teenager el/ la adolescente
telegram el telegrama
telephone el teléfono
telephone directory la guía telefónica
television la televisión
temperature la temperatura
tennis el tenis
tent la tienda de campaña

ENGLISH-SPANISH

terrible terrible
terrific estupendo
than: uglier than más feo que
thank agradecer
thank you gracias
that (*adjective*) ese, esa, aquel, aquella; (*pronoun*) eso, aquello; **I think that ...** pienso que ...; **that one** ése, ésa, aquél, aquella (*see grammar*)
the el, la, los, las (*see grammar*)
theatre el teatro
their su (*see grammar*)
theirs suyo (*see grammar*)
them les, las, ellos, ellas (*see grammar*)
then entonces
there allí; **there is/are** hay
thermometer el termómetro
thermos flask el termo
these (*adjective*) estos, estas; (*pronoun*) éstos, éstas (*see grammar*)
they ellos, ellas (*see grammar*)
thick grueso
thief el ladrón
thigh el muslo
thin delgado
thing la cosa
think pensar; **I don't think so** creo que no
thirsty: I'm thirsty tengo sed
this (*adjective*) este, esta; (*pronoun*) esto; **this one** éste, ésta (*see grammar*)
those (*adjective*) esos, esas, aquellos, aquellas; (*pronoun*) ésos, ésas, aquellos, aquellas (*see grammar*)
thread el hilo
throat la garganta

throat pastilles las pastillas para la garganta
through por
throw tirar
throw away tirar
thunder el trueno
thunderstorm la tormenta
Thursday jueves
ticket el billete; (*theatre*) la entrada
ticket office la taquilla
tide la marea
tie la corbata
tight ajustado
tights los panties
time el tiempo; (*occasion*) la vez; **what time is it?** ¿qué hora es?; **on time** a tiempo; **next time** la próxima vez
timetable el horario
tin opener el abrelatas
tip la propina
tired cansado
tissues los kleenex (R)
to a
toast (*bread*) la tostada
tobacco el tabaco
today hoy
toe el dedo del pie
together juntos
toilet los servicios
toilet paper el papel higiénico
tomato el tomate
tomato juice el zumo de tomate
tomorrow mañana; **the day after tomorrow** pasado mañana
tongue la lengua
tonight esta noche
tonsillitis las anginas
too: too big demasiado

grande; **me too** yo
también; **not too much** no
demasiado
tool la herramienta
tooth el diente
toothache el dolor de muelas
toothbrush el cepillo de
dientes
toothpaste la pasta de dientes
top: at the top en lo alto; **on
top of** encima de
torch la linterna
touch tocar
tourist el/la turista
towel la toalla
tower la torre
town la ciudad
toy el juguete
tracksuit el chandal
tradition la tradición
traditional tradicional
traffic el tráfico
traffic jam el
embotellamiento
traffic lights los semáforos
traffic warden el guardia de
tráfico
trailer (*behind car*) el
remolque
train el tren
trainers las playeras
translate traducir
travel viajar
travel agent's la agencia de
viajes
traveller's cheque el cheque
de viaje
tray la bandeja
tree el árbol
trip la excursión
trolley el carrito
trousers los pantalones
true verdadero

try intentar
try on probarse
T-shirt la camiseta
Tuesday martes
tuna fish el atún
tunnel el túnel
turkey el pavo
turn girar
tweezers las pinzas
twins los gemelos
typewriter la máquina de
escribir
tyre el neumático

ugly feo
umbrella el paraguas
uncle el tío
under debajo de
underdone demasiado poco
hecho
underground el metro
underneath (*adverb*) debajo
underpants los calzoncillos
understand entender
underwear la ropa interior
unemployed en paro
unfortunately
desgraciadamente
United States los Estados
Unidos
university la universidad
unpack deshacer las maletas
unpleasant desagradable
until hasta (que)
up arriba
upstairs arriba
urgent urgente

us nos, nosotros (*see grammar*)
use usar
useful útil
usual habitual
usually normalmente

vaccination la vacuna
vacuum cleaner la aspiradora
vagina la vagina
valid válido
valley el valle
valve la válvula
van la furgoneta
vanilla la vainilla
vase el jarrón
VD la enfermedad venérea
veal la ternera
vegetables las verduras
vegetarian vegetariano
vehicle el vehículo
very muy; **very much** mucho
vet el veterinario
video el vídeo
video recorder el vídeo
view la vista
viewfinder el visor
villa el chalet
village el pueblo
vinegar el vinagre
vineyard el viñedo
visa el visado
visit la visita
visit (*verb*) visitar
vitamins las vitaminas
voice la voz

waist la cintura
wait esperar
waiter el camarero
waiting room la sala de espera
waitress la camarera
wake (up) (*someone*) despertar; (*oneself*) despertarse
Wales Gales *m*
walk (*verb*) ir a pie
walk el paseo; **go for a walk** ir de paseo
walkman (R) el walkman (R)
wall la pared
wallet el monedero
want querer
war la guerra
warm caliente; **it's warm** hace calor
wash lavar; (*oneself*) lavarse
washbasin el lavabo
washing: do the washing lavar la ropa
washing machine la lavadora
washing powder el jabón en polvo
washing-up: do the washing up fregar los platos
washing-up liquid el detergente lavavajillas
wasp la avispa
watch (*for time*) el reloj
watch (*verb*) mirar
water el agua *f*
waterfall la cascada
waterski el esquí acuático
wave (*of water*) la ola

way: this way (*like this*) de esta manera; **can you tell me the way to ...?** ¿puede decirme por dónde se va a ...?

we nosotros, nosotras (*see grammar*)

weak débil

weather el tiempo; **the weather is good** hace buen tiempo

weather forecast el pronóstico del tiempo

wedding la boda

Wednesday miércoles

week la semana

weekend el fin de semana

weight el peso

welcome! ¡bienvenido!

well bien; **he's well/ not well** se/ no se siente bien

well done (*meat*) muy hecho

wellingtons las botas de agua

Welsh galés

west el oeste; **west of the town** al oeste de la ciudad

wet mojado

what? ¿qué?; **what is this?** ¿qué es esto?

wheel la rueda

wheelchair la silla de ruedas

when cuando; **when?** ¿cuándo?

where donde; **where?** ¿dónde?

which que; **which?** ¿cuál?

while mientras

whipped cream la nata batida

whisky el whisky

white blanco

who: who? ¿quién?; **the person who** la persona que

whole (*complete*) todo

whooping cough la tosferina

whose: whose is this? ¿de quién es esto?

why por qué

wide ancho

widow la viuda

widower el viudo

wife la mujer

wild salvaje

win ganar

wind el viento

window la ventana

windscreen el parabrisas

windscreen wiper el limpiaparabrisas

wine el vino; **red/ white/ rosé wine** el vino tinto/ blanco/ rosado

wine list la carta de vinos

wing el ala *f*

winter el invierno

wire el alambre

wish: best wishes saludos

with con; **with me** conmigo (*see grammar*)

without sin

witness testigo

woman la mujer

wonderful estupendo

wood la madera; (*forest*) el bosque

wool la lana

word la palabra

work el trabajo

work (*verb*) trabajar; **it's not working** no funciona

world el mundo

worry (*noun*) la preocupación

worry about preocuparse por

worse peor

worst peor

wound la herida

wrap envolver

ENGLISH-SPANISH

wrapping paper el papel de
   envolver
wrench la llave inglesa
wrist la muñeca
write escribir
writing paper el papel de
   escribir
wrong equivocado

zero cero
zip la cremallera
zoo el zoo

x-ray la radiografía

yacht el yate
year el año
yellow amarillo
yes sí
yesterday ayer
yet: not yet todavía no
yoghurt el yogur
you tú, te, Usted, Ustedes,
   vosotros, vosotras (*see*
   grammar)
young joven
young people los jóvenes
your tu, su, vuestro (*see*
   grammar)
yours tuyo, suyo, vuestro (*see*
   grammar)
youth hostel el albergue de
   juventud

Note that in Spanish-English dictionaries, 'ch' comes after 'cu' and 'll' comes after 'lu'.

a: voy a Madrid/ la estación I'm going to Madrid/ the station; **a las tres** at 3 o'clock; **a la semana** per week; **a 2 Km.** 2 km away
abajo downstairs
abeja f bee
abierto open
abogado m lawyer
abrebotellas m bottle-opener
abrelatas m tin-opener
abrigo m coat
abril April
abrir open
abuela f grandmother
abuelo m grandfather
aburrido boring
acabar finish; **acabo de comer** I've just eaten
acantilado m cliff
accidente m accident
aceite m oil
aceite de oliva m olive oil
aceituna f olive
acelerador m accelerator
acento m accent
aceptar accept
acera f pavement

ácido sour
acompañar accompany
acondicionador de pelo m conditioner
aconsejar advise
acordarse remember
acostarse go to bed
acuerdo: estoy de acuerdo I agree
adaptador m adaptor
adelantado: por adelantado in advance
adelantar overtake; **¡adelante!** come in!
adentro inside
adiós goodbye
adolescente m/f teenager
aduana f customs
adulto m adult
aeromozo m steward
aeropuerto m airport
afeitarse shave
afortunadamente fortunately
afueras fpl suburbs
agencia f agency
agencia de viajes f travel agent's
agenda f diary
agosto August
agradable pleasant
agradecer thank
agradecido m grateful
agresivo aggressive
agua f water; **agua potable** drinking water
agua de colonia f eau de toilette
agua mineral f mineral water

SPANISH-ENGLISH

aguantar: no aguanto el queso I can't stand cheese
aguja f needle
agujero m hole
ahora now
aire acondicionado m air-conditioning
ajo m garlic
ajustado tight
ala f wing
alambre m wire
alarma f alarm
albaricoque m apricot
albergue de juventud m youth hostel
alcohol m alcohol
alegre happy
alemán German
Alemania f Germany
alérgico a allergic to
alfiler m pin
alfombra f rug
algas fpl seaweed
algo something; **algo más** something else
algodón m cotton, cotton wool
alguien somebody
algún, alguno some; any
alicates mpl pliers
aliñada with salad dressing
almendra f almond
almohada f pillow
almuerzo m lunch
alojamiento m accommodation
alquilar rent; hire
alquiler m rent
alquiler de coches m car rental
alrededor (de) around
alternador m alternator
alto high; tall; **de 2 metros de**

alto 2 m high; **en lo alto** at the top
allá: más allá further
allí there
amable kind
amamantar breastfeed
amargo bitter
amarillo yellow
ambulancia f ambulance
a menudo often
América f America
americano American
amigo m, **amiga** f friend
amor m love; **hacer el amor** make love
amortiguador m shock-absorber
amperio m: **de 15 amperios** 15-amp
ampliación f enlargement
ampolla f blister
ancla f anchor
ancho wide
andar walk; go
andén m platform
angina (de pecho) f angina
anginas fpl tonsillitis; tonsils
anillo m ring
animal m animal
aniversario de boda m wedding anniversary
anorak m anorak
ante m suede
antepasado m ancestor
antes (de) before
antibiótico m antibiotic
anticonceptivo m contraceptive
anticongelante m antifreeze
antigüedad f: **una tienda de antigüedades** an antique shop
antiguo ancient

antihistamínico *m*
    antihistamine
antiséptico antiseptic
anular cancel
año *m* year
Año Nuevo *m* New Year
apagar switch off
apagón *m* power cut
aparato *m* device
aparcamiento *m* car park
aparcar park
apartamento *m* apartment
apellido *m* surname
apendicitis *f* appendicitis
aperitivo *m* aperitif
apetecer: me apetece I feel
    like
apetito *m* appetite
apodo *m* nickname
apoplejía *f* stroke
aprender learn
aproximadamente about
aquel, aquella that (*see
    grammar*)
aquí here
árabe Arabic
araña *f* spider
árbol *m* tree
arco iris *m* rainbow
arena *f* sand
armario *m* cupboard
arqueología *f* archaeology
arreglar mend
arriba up; upstairs
arroyo *m* stream
arroz *m* rice
arte *m* art
artesanía *f* crafts
artificial artificial
artista *m/f* artist
asar roast
ascensor *m* lift
aseos *mpl* toilets

asiento *m* seat
asma *f* asthma
aspiradora *f* hoover (R)
aspirina *f* aspirin
atajo *m* shortcut
ataque *m* attack; **ataque al
    corazón** heart attack
atascado stuck
aterrizar land
Atlántico *m* Atlantic
atractivo attractive
atrás: la parte de atrás   the
    back
atreverse dare
atropellar knock over
atún *m* tuna fish
audífono *m* hearing aid
aún even
aunque although
Australia *f* Australia
autobús *m* bus
automático automatic
automovilista *m/f* car driver
autopista *f* motorway
autoservicio *m* self-service
autostop *m* hitchhiking;
    hacer autostop hitchhike
avellana *f* hazelnut
avería *f* breakdown
averiarse break down
aves *fpl* poultry
avión *m* aeroplane; **por
    avión** by airmail
avisar inform
avispa *f* wasp
ayer yesterday
ayuda *f* help
ayudar help
ayuntamiento *m* town hall
azafata *f* air hostess
azúcar *m* sugar
azul blue

SPANISH-ENGLISH

 B

baca f roof rack
bailar dance
bajar go down
bajarse get off
bajo low; short
balcón m balcony
banco m bank; bench
bandeja f tray
bandera f flag
bañarse go swimming; have a bath
bañera f bathtub
baño m bath
bar m bar
barato cheap
barba f beard
barbacoa f barbecue
barbero m barber
barbilla f chin
barca de remos f rowing boat
barco m boat
barco de vela m sailing boat
barra de labios f lipstick
bastante enough
basura f litter
bata f dressing gown
batería f battery
bebé m baby
beber drink
bebida f drink
beige beige
Bélgica f Belgium
berenjena f aubergine
beso m kiss
betún m shoe polish
biblioteca f library
bicicleta f bicycle
bien well; right
¡bienvenido! welcome!

bifurcación f fork
bigote m moustache
billete m ticket; **billete de ida** single ticket; **billete de ida y vuelta** return ticket
billete de banco m banknote
blanco white
blusa f blouse
boca f mouth
bocadillo m sandwich
bocina f horn
boda f wedding
bodega f wine cellar
bolígrafo m biro (R)
bolsa f bag
bolsa de agua caliente f hot-water bottle
bolsillo m pocket
bolso m handbag
bollo m roll
bomba f bomb
bomberos mpl fire brigade
bombilla f light bulb
bombona de gas f Calor gas (R)
bonito nice
bonito m tuna fish
borracho drunk
bosque m forest
bota f boot
botas de agua fpl wellingtons
botella f bottle
botiquín m first aid kit
botón m button
boya f buoy
bragas fpl panties
brazo m arm
británico British
brocha de afeitar f shaving brush
broche m brooch
bronceado m suntan
brújula f compass

buceo *m* skin-diving
bueno good
bufanda *f* scarf
bujía *f* spark plug
burro *m* donkey
buscar look for
buzón *m* letterbox

caballo *m* horse
caballero gentleman;
  caballeros gents
cabeza *f* head
cabina telefónica *f* phone
  box
cable alargador *m* extension
  lead
cabra *f* goat
cacahuetes *mpl* peanuts
cacao *m* cocoa
cada every
cadena *f* chain
cadera *f* hip
caer drop; **caerse** fall
café *m* coffee; **café con leche**
  white coffee; **café solo**
  black coffee
cafetería *f* café
caja *f* box; cash desk
caja de cambios *f* gearbox
cajero automático *m* cash
  dispenser
calambre *m* cramp
calcetines *mpl* socks
calculadora *f* calculator
calefacción *f* heating
calefacción central *f* central
  heating
calendario *m* calendar
calidad *f* quality

caliente hot
calmante *m* painkiller;
  tranquillizer
calor *m* heat; **hace calor** it's
  warm/ hot
calvo bald
calzoncillos *mpl* underpants
calle *f* street
cama *f* bed; **cama
  individual** single bed;
  cama de matrimonio
  double bed
cama de campaña *f* campbed
cámara *f* camera; inner tube
camarera *f* waitress;
  chambermaid
camarero *m* waiter
camarote *m* cabin
cambiar change
cambiarse (de ropa) get
  changed
cambio *m* exchange; small
  change; **tipo de cambio**
  exchange rate
camino *m* path
camión *m* lorry
camisa *f* shirt
camiseta *f* T-shirt
camisón *m* nightdress
campana *f* bell
camping *m* camping;
  campsite
campo *m* countryside;
  football ground
canadiense Canadian
canal de la Mancha *m*
  Channel
cancelar cancel
canción *f* song
cangrejo *m* crab
cangura *f* baby-sitter
cansado tired
cantar sing

capaz: ser capaz (de) be able to

capazo m carry-cot

capitán m captain

capó m bonnet

cara f face

caramelo m sweet

caravana f caravan; traffic jam

carburador m carburettor

cárcel f prison

cardenal m bruise

carne f meat; **carne de vaca** beef; **carne de cerdo** pork

carne picada f minced meat

carnet de conducir m driving licence

carnet de identidad m identity card

carnicería f butcher's

caro expensive

carretera f road

carta f letter; menu

carta de vinos f wine list

cartel m poster

cartera f briefcase; wallet

carterista m pickpocket

cartero m postman

cartón m cardboard

casa f house; **en casa** at home; **en casa de José** at José's

casa de huéspedes f guesthouse

casado married

cascada f waterfall

casi almost

cassette f cassette

cassette m cassette player

castaña f chestnut

castillo m castle

casualidad f: **por casualidad** by chance

catarro m: **tengo catarro** I've got a cold

catedral f cathedral

católico Catholic

causa f cause

caza f game (*meat*); hunting

cazo m saucepan

cebolla f onion

ceja f eyebrow

celoso jealous

cementerio m cemetery

cena f dinner

cenar have dinner

cenicero m ashtray

centígrado centigrade

centro m centre

centro comercial m shopping centre

cepillo m brush

cepillo de dientes m toothbrush

cerca (de) near

cerdo m pork; pig

cereza f cherry

cerilla f match

cero zero

cerrado closed

cerradura f lock

cerrar close; **cerrar con llave** lock

cerrojo m bolt; **echar el cerrojo** bolt

certificado m certificate

cerveza f beer

césped m lawn

cesta f basket

ciclista m/f cyclist

ciego blind

cielo m sky

ciencia f science

cigala f crayfish

cigarrillo m cigarette

cigarro m cigar

cine *m* cinema
cinta *f* tape
cintura *f* waist
cinturón *m* belt
cinturón de seguridad *m* seat belt
ciruela *f* plum
cita *f* appointment
ciudad *f* town
claro clear; azul claro light blue
clase *f* class
clavo *m* nail
clima *m* climate
cobrador *m* conductor
cocer al horno bake
cocina *f* kitchen; cooker
cocinero *m* cook
cóctel *m* cocktail
coche *m* car
coche-cama *m* sleeper
coche-comedor *m* dining car
cochecito *m* pram
codígo de la circulación *m* highway code
codo *m* elbow
coger catch; take
col *f* cabbage
cola *f* tail; queue; hacer cola queue
colchón *m* mattress
colegio *m* school
colección *f* collection
colegio *m* school
coles de Bruselas *fpl* Brussels sprouts
coliflor *f* cauliflower
colina *f* hill
color *m* colour
collar *m* necklace
comedor *m* dining room
comer eat
comida *f* food; meal; lunch

comisaría *f* police station
como as; like; ¿cómo? how?; ¿cómo está? how are you?; ¿cómo dice? pardon?
compañía *f* company
compañía aérea *f* airline
compartimento *m* compartment
compartir share
complicado complicated
comprar buy
compras *fpl*: ir de compras go shopping
compresa *m* sanitary towel
computadora *f* computer
con with
concierto *m* concert
concha *f* shell
condón *m* condom
conducir drive
conductor *m* driver
conejo *m* rabbit
confirmar confirm
congelado frozen
congelador *m* freezer
conmigo with me
conocer know
conserje *m* porter
consigna *f* left luggage
consulado *m* consulate
contacto *m*: ponerse en contacto con contact
contado: pagar al contado pay cash
contaminado polluted
contar count; tell
contento happy
contigo with you
contra against
contraventanas *fpl* shutters
coñac *m* brandy
copa *f* cup
coquetear flirt

corazón *m* heart
corbata *f* tie
cordero *m* lamb
cordones de los zapatos *mpl* shoe laces
correa del ventilador *f* fan belt
correcto correct
correo *m* mail
correos *m* post office
correr run
cortadura *f* cut
cortar cut
cortauñas *m* nail clippers
corte de pelo *m* haircut
cortina *f* curtain
corto short
cosa *f* thing
coser sew
cosméticos *mpl* cosmetics
costa *f* coast
costar cost
costilla *f* rib
costumbre *f* custom
cráneo *m* skull
crecer grow
creer believe
crema base *f* foundation cream
crema de belleza *f* cold cream
crema limpiadora *f* cleansing cream
cremallera *f* zip
crêpe *f* pancake
crisis nerviosa *f* nervous breakdown
cristal *m* crystal; glass
cruce *f* junction; crossing
crucero *m* cruise
crudo raw
cuadro *m* painting
cual which; who

¿cuándo? when?
¿cuánto? how much?; **en cuanto ...** as soon as ...
¿cuántos? how many?
cuaderno *m* notebook
cuarto quarter
cuarto de baño *m* bathroom
cuarto de estar *m* sitting room
cubierta *f* deck
cubiertos *mpl* cutlery
cubito de hielo *m* ice cube
cubo *m* bucket
cubo de la basura *m* dustbin
cucaracha *f* cockroach
cuchara *f* spoon
cucharilla *f* teaspoon
cuchilla de afeitar *f* razor blade
cuchillo *m* knife
cuello *m* neck; collar
cuenco *m* bowl
cuenta *f* bill
cuerda *f* rope; string
cuero *m* leather
cuerpo *m* body
cueva *f* cave
¡cuidado! look out!; **¡tenga cuidado!** be careful!
culebra *f* snake
culpa *f*: **es culpa mía/ suya** it's my/ his fault
cumpleaños *m* birthday; **¡feliz cumpleaños!** happy birthday!
cuna *f* cot
cura *m* priest
curva *f* bend
chalet *m* villa
champiñones *mpl* mushrooms
champú *m* shampoo
chandal *m* tracksuit

chaqueta *f* cardigan; jacket
chárter: el vuelo chárter *m* charter flight
cheque *m* cheque
cheque de viaje *m* traveller's cheque
chica *f* girl
chicle *m* chewing gum
chico *m* boy
chiste *m* joke
chocolate *m* chocolate; **chocolate con leche/ de hacer** milk/ plain chocolate; **chocolate caliente** hot chocolate
chubasquero *m* cagoule
chuleta *f* chop
chupa-chups *m* (R) lollipop

dar give
de of; from
debajo underneath; **debajo de** under
deber: **debo ir** I must go
débil weak
decidir decide
decir say
dedo *m* finger
dedo del pie *m* toe
defectuoso faulty
dejar leave; let; **dejar de beber** stop drinking
delante de in front of
delantero: **la parte delantera** the front
delgado thin
delicioso delicious

demás: **los demás** the others
demasiado too; too much
dentadura postiza *f* dentures
dentro (de) inside
dentista *m* dentist
depender: **depende** it depends
dependiente *m* shop assistant
deporte *m* sport
depósito *m* tank
deprimido depressed
derecha *f* right; **a la derecha (de)** on the right (of)
derecho: **todo derecho** straight ahead; **tener derecho** have the right
desafortunadamente unfortunately
desagradable unpleasant
desaparecer disappear
desastre *m* disaster
desayuno *m* breakfast
descansar rest
desde (que) since
deshacer las maletas unpack
desinfectante *m* disinfectant
desmayarse faint
desnudo naked
desodorante *m* deodorant
despacio slowly
despedirse say goodbye
despertador *m* alarm clock
despertar wake
despertarse wake up
despierto awake
después afterwards; **después de** after
destornillador *m* screwdriver
detener arrest; stop
detergente lavavajillas *m* washing-up liquid
detrás (de) behind

devolver give back; **voy a devolver** I'm going to be sick

día *m* day; **buenos días** good morning; hello

diabético diabetic

dialecto *m* dialect

diamante *m* diamond

diapositiva *f* slide

diario daily

diario *m* diary; newspaper

diarrea *f* diarrhoea

diccionario *m* dictionary

diciembre December

diente *m* tooth

dieta *f* diet

diferente different

difícil difficult

dinero *m* money

Dios *m* God

dirección *f* direction; address; steering

directo direct

disco *m* record

disco compacto *m* compact disc

discoteca *f* disco

disculparse apologize

distancia *f* distance

distinto different

divertido entertaining; funny

distribuidor *m* distributor

divertirse have a good time

divorciado divorced

doble double

documento *m* document

doler hurt; **me duele aquí** it hurts here

dolor *m* pain; **dolor de muelas/cabeza** toothache/headache; **dolor de garganta** sore throat

doloroso painful

domingo Sunday

donde where

dormido asleep

dormir sleep

dormitorio *m* bedroom

droga *f* drug

ducha *f* shower

dudar doubt

dulce sweet

dunas *fpl* sand dunes

durante during

duro hard

E

echar throw; **echar al buzón** post; **echo de menos a** I miss

edad *f* age

edad media *f* Middle Ages

edificio *m* building

edredón *m* quilt

educado polite

eje *m* axle

eje del cigüeñal *m* crankshaft

ejemplo *m* example; **por ejemplo** for example

el the (*see grammar*)

él he; him (*see grammar*)

elástico elastic

electricidad *f* electricity

eléctrico electric

elegir choose

ella she; her (*see grammar*)

ellas they; them (*see grammar*)

ellos they; them (*see grammar*)

embajada *f* embassy

embarazada pregnant

embotellamiento *m* traffic

jam
embrague *m* clutch
embudo *m* funnel
emergencia *f* emergency
emocionante exciting
empaste *m* filling
empezar begin
empinado steep
empleado *m*, **empleada** *f*
  employee; shop assistant
empujar push
en in; on; **en la estación** at
  the station; **en coche** by car
encantador lovely
encendedor *m* lighter
encender light; switch on
encendido *m* ignition
encima above; **encima (de)**
  on (top of)
encontrar find
enchufe *m* plug
enero January
enfadado angry
enfermedad *f* disease
enfermedad venérea *f* VD
enfermera *f* nurse
enfermo ill
enfrente (de) opposite
¡enhorabuena!
  congratulations!
enlace *m* connection
ensalada *f* salad
enseñar teach; show
entender understand
entero whole
entonces then
entrada *f* entrance; ticket
entrar go in
entre among; between
entremés *m* starter
entrevista *f* interview;
  meeting
enviar send

envolver wrap up
epiléptico epileptic
equipaje *m* luggage
equipaje de mano *m* hand
  luggage
equipo *m* team
equitación *f* horse riding
equivocado wrong
error *m* mistake
escaleras *fpl* stairs
escandaloso shocking
escarcha *f* frost
escoba *f* broom
escocés Scottish
Escocia *f* Scotland
esconder hide
escribir write
escuchar listen
escuela *f* school
ese, esa that (*see grammar*)
ése, ésa that one (*see
  grammar*)
esmalte de uñas *m* nail polish
eso that; **eso es** that's it,
  that's right
esos, esas those (*see grammar*)
espalda *f* back
España *f* Spain
español Spanish
español *m* Spaniard
española *f* Spanish woman/
  girl
espárragos *mpl* asparagus
especia *f* spice
especialidad *f* speciality
especialmente especially
espejo *m* mirror
esperar wait; hope
espina *f* fishbone
espinacas *fpl* spinach
espuma de afeitar *f* shaving
  foam
esquí *m* ski; skiing

SPANISH-ENGLISH

esquí acuático *m* waterski; waterskiing
esquina *f* corner
estación *f* station
estación de autobuses *f* bus station
Estados Unidos *mpl* United States
estanco *m* tobacconist's
estanque *m* pond
estar be (*see grammar*)
este *m* east
este, esta this (*see grammar*)
éste, ésta this one (*see grammar*)
esto this
estómago *m* stomach
estos, estas these (*see grammar*)
éstos, éstas these ones (*see grammar*)
estrecho narrow
estrella *f* star
estreñido constipated
estropear damage
estudiante *m/f* student
estudiar study
estupendo wonderful
estúpido stupid
etiqueta *f* label
eurocheque *m* Eurocheque
Europa *f* Europe
europeo European
evidente obvious
excelente excellent
excepto except
exceso de equipaje *m* excess baggage
excursión *f* trip
explicar explain
exposición *f* exhibition
expreso special delivery; express

extintor *m* fire extinguisher
extranjero foreign
extranjero *m* foreigner; **en el extranjero** abroad
extraño strange

F

fábrica *f* factory
fabricación *f*: **de fabricación casera** homemade
fácil easy
factura *f* bill; invoice
falda *f* skirt
falso false
familia *f* family
famoso famous
farmacia *f* chemist's
faro *m* lighthouse; light
faros *mpl* headlights
favorito favourite
febrero February
fecha *f* date
feo ugly
ferias *fpl* fair
ferretería *f* ironmonger's
ferrocarril *m* railway
ferry *m* ferry
festividad *f* celebration
fiebre *f* fever
fiebre del heno *f* hay fever
fiesta *f* public holiday; party
filete *m* steak; fillet
filtro *m* filter
fin *f* end; **por fin** at last
final *m* end
fin de semana *m* weekend
fino fine
fino *m* type of sherry
firma *f* signature; firm
firmar sign

flaco skinny
flash *m* flash
flor *f* flower
florero *m* vase
floristería *f* florist
folleto *m* leaflet
fondo *m* bottom; **en el fondo (de)** at the bottom (of)
fontanero *m* plumber
footing *m*: **hago footing** I go jogging
forma *f* form; **en forma** fit
fotografía *f* photograph
fotografiar photograph
fotógrafo *m* photographer
fotómetro *m* light meter
fractura *f* fracture
frambuesa *f* raspberry
francés French
Francia *f* France
fregar: fregar los platos do the washing up
fregadero *m* sink
freír fry
frenar brake
freno *m* brake
freno de mano *m* handbrake
frente *f* forehead
fresa *f* strawberry
fresco fresh
frigorífico *m* fridge
frío cold; **hace frío** it's cold
frontera *f* border
fruta *f* fruit
fuego *m* fire; **¿tiene fuego?** have you got a light?
fuegos artificiales *mpl* fireworks
fuente *f* fountain
fuera outside
fuerte strong; loud
fumadores smoking
fumar smoke

funcionar: no funciona it's not working
funeral *m* funeral
furgoneta *f* van
furioso furious
fusible *m* fuse
fútbol *m* football
frutería *f* greengrocer
futuro *m* future

gabardina *f* raincoat
gafas *fpl* glasses
gafas de sol *fpl* sunglasses
galés Welsh
Gales *m* Wales
galleta *f* biscuit
gamba *f* prawn
ganar win
ganso *m* goose
garaje *m* garage
garantía *f* guarantee
garganta *f* throat
gas *m* gas; **con gas** fizzy
gas-oil *m* diesel
gasolina *f* petrol
gasolinera *f* petrol station
gastar spend
gato *m* cat; jack
gaviota *f* seagull
gemelos *mpl* twins
gente *f* people
genuino genuine
gerente *m* manager
ginebra *f* gin
girar turn
gitano *m* gypsy
gobierno *m* government
golpear hit
goma *f* rubber; glue

goma elástica *f* rubber band
gordo fat
gorra *f* cap
gorro de baño *m* bathing cap
gota *f* drop
gotera *f* leak
gracias thank you
gracioso funny
gramática *f* grammar
Gran Bretaña *f* Great Britain
grande big
grandes almacenes *mpl* department store
granizo *m* hail
granja *f* farm
granjero *m* farmer
grano *m* spot
grasa *f* fat
grasiento greasy
gratis free
Grecia *f* Greece
griego Greek
grifo *m* tap
gripe *f* flu
gris grey
gritar shout
grosero rude
grueso thick
grupo *m* group
grupo sanguíneo *m* blood group
guantes *mpl* gloves
guapo handsome
guardar keep; put away
guardaropa *m* cloakroom
guerra *f* war
guía *m* guide
guía telefónica *f* phone book
guisantes *mpl* peas
guisar cook
guitarra *f* guitar
gustar: me gusta el queso/ comer I like cheese/ eating

gusto: mucho gusto pleased to meet you!

H

habitación *f* room; **habitación individual/ doble** single/ double room
hablar speak
hacer make; do; **hace tres días** three days ago
hacerse become
hacia towards
hacha *m* axe
hambre *f*: **tengo hambre** I'm hungry
hamburguesa *f* hamburger
harina *f* flour
harto: estoy harto (de) I'm fed up (with)
hasta even; **hasta (que)** until; **hasta mañana** see you tomorrow; **hasta luego** see you
hay there is/ are
hecho: demasiado hecho overdone; **bien hecho** well done; **poco hecho** rare; **demasiado poco hecho** underdone
hecho *m* fact
helado *m* ice cream; **estoy helado** I'm freezing
hemorroides *fpl* piles
herida *f* wound
herido injured
hermana *f* sister
hermano *m* brother
hermoso beautiful
hervir boil

hidratante: crema hidratante *f* moisturizer
hielo *m* ice
hierba *f* grass
hierbas *fpl* herbs
hierro *m* iron
hígado *m* liver
hija *f* daughter
hijo *m* son
hilo *m* thread
hipo *m* hiccups
historia *f* history; story
hoja *f* leaf
¡hola! hello
Holanda *f* Holland
holandés Dutch
hombre *m* man
hombro *m* shoulder
honrado honest
hora *f* hour; **¿qué hora es?** what time is it?
horario *m* timetable
hormiga *f* ant
horno *m* oven
horrible horrible
hospedarse stay
hospital *m* hospital
hospitalidad *f* hospitality
hotel *m* hotel
hoy today
huelga *f* strike
hueso *m* bone
huevera *f* egg cup
huevo *m* egg; **huevo duro/ pasado por agua** hard-boiled/ boiled egg; **huevos revueltos** scrambled eggs
húmedo damp
humo *m* smoke
humor *m* humour
hundirse sink

idea *f* idea
idioma *m* language
idiota *m/f* idiot
igual equal; like; **me da igual** it's all the same to me
iglesia *f* church
imperdible *m* safety pin
importante important
importar: no importa it doesn't matter; **¿le importa si ...?** do you mind if ...?
imposible impossible
impreso *m* form
impresos *mpl* printed matter
incluido included; **todo incluido** all inclusive
incluso even
increíble incredible
independiente independent
indicador *m* indicator
indicador de nivel *m* gauge
indigestión *f* indigestion
industria *f* industry
infarto *m* heart attack
infección *f* infection
inflamado swollen
información *f* information
Inglaterra *f* England
inglés English
inglés *m* Englishman
inglesa *f* Englishwoman; English girl
inmediatamente immediately
inocente innocent
insecto *m* insect
insolación *f* sunstroke
insomnio *m* insomnia

SPANISH-ENGLISH

instrumento musical *m* musical instrument
inteligente intelligent
intentar try
interesante interesting
interruptor *m* switch
intoxicación alimenticia *f* food poisoning
invierno *m* winter
invitación *f* invitation
invitado *m* guest
invitar invite
inyección *f* injection
ir go
irse go away; **¡váyase!** go away!
Irlanda *f* Ireland
Irlanda del Norte *f* Northern Ireland
irlandés Irish
isla *f* island
Italia *f* Italy
italiano Italian
izquierda *f* left; **a la izquierda (de)** on the left (of)

joven young
joyas *fpl* jewellery
joyería *f* jeweller's
judías *fpl* beans; **judías verdes** green beans
judío Jewish
juego *m* game
jueves Thursday
jugar play
juguete *m* toy
julio July
junio June
junto (a) next (to)
juntos together

kilo *m* kilo
kilómetro *m* kilometre
kiosko de periódicos *m* newsstand
kleenex *mpl* (R) tissues

jabón *m* soap
jabón en polvo *m* washing powder
jamón *m* ham
jardín *m* garden
jarra *f* jug
jarrón *m* vase
jazz *m* jazz
jefe *m* boss
jerez *m* sherry
jersey *m* jumper
¡Jesús! bless you!

la the; her; it (*see grammar*)
labio *m* lip
laca *f* hair spray
lado *m* side; **al lado de** next to
ladrillo *m* brick
ladrón *m* thief
lagartija *f* lizard
lágrima *f* tear (*crying*)
lago *m* lake
lámpara *f* lamp
lana *f* wool
langosta *f* lobster

lápiz *m* pencil
lapíz de ojos *m* eyeliner
largo long
las the; them (*see grammar*)
lástima *f*: **es una lástima** it's a
  pity
lata *f* can, tin
lavabo *m* washbasin
lavadora *f* washing machine
lavandería automática *f*
  launderette
lavar wash; **lavar la ropa** do
  the washing
lavarse wash
laxante *m* laxative
le him; her; you (*see grammar*)
lección *f* lesson
leche *f* milk
leche limpiadora *f* skin
  cleanser
lechería *f* dairy
lechuga *f* lettuce
leer read
lejía *f* bleach
lejos far away; **más lejos**
  further away
lengua *f* tongue; language
lentillas *fpl* contact lenses
lentillas blandas *fpl* soft
  lenses
lentillas duras *fpl* hard lenses
lentillas porosas *fpl* gas
  permeable lenses
lento slow
les them; you (*see grammar*)
levantarse get up
ley *f* law
libra *f* pound
libre free
libre de impuestos duty-free
librería *f* bookshop
libreta de direcciones *f*
  address book

libro *m* book
libro de frases *m* phrase
  book
licor *m* liqueur
ligero light
lima de uñas *f* nailfile
límite de velocidad *m* speed
  limit
limón *m* lemon
limonada *f* lemonade
limpiaparabrisas *m*
  windscreen wiper
limpiar clean
limpio clean
linterna *f* torch
lío *m* mess
lista *f* list
lista de Correos *f* poste
  restante
listo clever; ready
litera *f* couchette
literas *fpl* bunk beds
litro *m* litre
lo it (*see grammar*)
loción antimosquitos *f*
  insect repellent
loción bronceadora *f* suntan
  lotion
loco mad
locomotora *f* engine
Londres London
longitud *f* length
los the (*see grammar*)
loza *f* crockery
luces de posición *fpl*
  sidelights
luces traseras *fpl* rear lights
luna *f* moon
lunes Monday
luz *f* light
llamada a cobro revertido *f*
  reverse charge call
llamar call; **me llamo**

Manuel my name is Manuel
llave *f* key
llave inglesa *f* spanner
llavero *m* key ring
llegada *f* arrival
llegar arrive; **llegar a** get to
lleno full; **lleno de ...** full of ...
llevar carry; take; give a lift to; wear
llevarse take away
llorar cry
llover rain; **está lloviendo** it's raining
lluvia *f* rain

M

machista *m* male chauvinist pig
machista sexist
madera *f* wood
madre *f* mother
maduro ripe
mal badly; **mal humor** bad temper
malentendido *m* misunderstanding
maleta *f* suitcase; **hacer las maletas** pack
maletero *m* boot (*of car*)
malo bad
mamá *f* mum
mancha *f* stain
mandíbula *f* jaw
manera *f*: **de esta manera** in this way
manga *f* sleeve
mano *f* hand; **de segunda mano** second-hand

manta *f* blanket
mantel *m* tablecloth
mantequilla *f* butter
manzana *f* apple
mañana *f* morning; **a las 5 de la mañana** at 5 a.m.
mañana (*adverb*) tomorrow
mapa *m* map
maquillaje *m* make-up
máquina de escribir *f* typewriter
máquina de fotos *f* camera
maquinilla de afeitar *f* razor
mar *m* sea
marcha *f* gear
marcha atrás *f* reverse gear
marcharse go away
marea *f* tide
mareado: estoy mareado I'm seasick
marido *m* husband
mariposa *f* butterfly
mariscos *mpl* seafood
marrón brown
martes Tuesday
martillo *m* hammer
marzo March
más more; **más de** more than; **más pequeño** smaller; **ya no más** no more; **el más caro** the most expensive
matar kill
matrícula *f* number plate
mayo May
mayonesa *f* mayonnaise
mayor adult; bigger; older; biggest; oldest; **la mayor parte (de)** most (of)
me me; myself (*see grammar*)
mecánico *m* mechanic
media hora *f* half an hour
medianoche *f* midnight

SPANISH-ENGLISH

medias *fpl* stockings
médico *m* doctor
medio: medio litro/ día half a litre/ day; **de tamaño medio** medium-sized
medio *m* middle
mediodía *m* midday
Mediterráneo *m* Mediterranean
medusa *f* jellyfish
mejillones *mpl* mussels
mejor best; better
mejorar improve
melocotón *m* peach
melón *m* melon
menos less; **por lo menos** at least
mercado *m* market
mermelada *f* jam; marmalade
mes *m* month
mesa *f* table
metro *m* meter; underground
mi my (*see grammar*)
mí me (*see grammar*)
miedo *m* fear; **tengo miedo (de/a)** I'm afraid (of)
miel *f* honey
mientras while
miércoles Wednesday
millón *m* million
minusválido disabled
mío, mía mine (*see grammar*)
minuto *m* minute
mirar look (at)
mis my (*see grammar*)
misa *f* mass
mismo same; **yo mismo/ tú mismo** myself/ yourself
mitad *f* half
mobylette *f* moped
mochila *f* rucksack
moda *f* fashion; **de moda** fashionable
moderno modern
mojado wet
molestar disturb; bother
molesto annoying
monedero *m* purse
montaña *f* mountain
mora *f* blackberry
morado purple
mordedura *f* bite
morir die
morriña *f*: **tengo morriña** I'm homesick
mosca *f* fly
mostaza *f* mustard
mostrador de facturación *m* check-in
mostrar show
moto *f* motorbike
motor *m* engine
motora *f* motorboat
mover move
muchedumbre *f* crowd
mucho much; a lot (of); very; **muchos países** many countries
muebles *mpl* furniture
muelle *m* spring; quay
muerte *f* death
muerto dead
mujer *f* woman; wife
muletas *fpl* crutches
multa *f* fine (*penalty*)
mundo *m* world
muñeca *f* wrist; doll
músculo *m* muscle
museo *m* museum
museo de arte *m* art gallery
música *f* music; **música clásica/ folklórica/ pop** classical/ folk/ pop music
muslo *m* thigh
muy very

nacido born
nacionalidad f nationality
nada nothing; **de nada** you're welcome
nadar swim
nadie nobody
naranja f orange
nariz m nose
nata f cream
nata batida f whipped cream
natación f swimming
natural natural
naturaleza f nature
náusea f: **siento náuseas** I feel sick
navaja f penknife
Navidad f Christmas
necesario necessary
necesitar: necesito I need
negativo m negative
negocio m business
negro black
nervioso nervous
neumático m tyre
neurótico neurotic
ni ... ni ... neither ... nor ...
niebla f fog
nieve f snow
ningún, ninguno nobody; none; not one; no ...; **en ningún sitio** nowhere
niñera f nanny
niño m, **niña** f child
no no; **no estoy cansado** I'm not tired; **no quiero** I don't want; **éste no** not this one
noche f night; **esta noche** tonight; **buenas noches** good night
nochebuena f Christmas Eve
nochevieja f New Year's Eve
nombre m name
nombre de pila m first name
nombre de soltera m maiden name
normal normal
normalmente normally
norte m north; **al norte de la ciudad** north of the town
nos us; ourselves (*see grammar*)
nosotros, nosotras we; us (*see grammar*)
noticias fpl news
novela f novel
novia f girlfriend; fiancée; bride
noviembre November
novio m boyfriend; fiancé; groom
nube f cloud
nublado cloudy
nuera f daughter-in-law
nuestro, nuestra our; ours (*see grammar*)
nuevo new
nuez f nut
número m number
número de teléfono m phone number
nunca never

o or; **o ... o ...** either ... or ...
obedecer obey
objetivo m lens; objective
obra f work; play (*in theatre*)

obras *fpl* roadworks
obstruido blocked
obturador *m* shutter
octubre October
ocupado engaged; busy
odiar hate
oeste *m* west; **al oeste de la ciudad** west of the town
ofender offend
oferta *f* offer
oficina *f* office
oficina de objetos perdidos *f* lost property office
oficio *m* job
ofrecer offer
oído *m* ear; hearing
oír hear
ojo *m* eye
ola *f* wave
oler smell
olor *m* smell
olvidar forget
ópera *f* opera
operación *f* operation
operadora *f* operator
Oporto *m* port (*wine*)
óptico *m* optician
optimista optimistic
oreja *f* ear
organizar organize
órgano *m* organ
orgulloso proud
orilla *f* shore
oro *m* gold
orquesta *f* orchestra
oscuro dark
ostra *f* oyster
otoño *m* autumn
otro another (one); **otros países** other countries; **otra vez** again; **el otro** the other (one)
oveja *f* sheep

padre *m* father
padres *mpl* parents
pagar pay
página *f* page
país *m* country
paisaje *m* scenery
pájaro *m* bird
pala *f* spade
palabra *f* word
palacio *m* palace
palanca de velocidades *f* gear lever
pan *m* bread; **pan blanco/ integral** white/ wholemeal bread
panadería *f* baker's
pantalones *mpl* trousers
pantalones cortos *mpl* shorts
panties *mpl* tights
pañal *m* nappy
paño de cocina *m* tea towel
pañuelo *m* handkerchief; scarf
papá *m* dad
papel *m* paper
papel celo *m* (R) sellotape (R)
papel de plata *m* silver foil
papel de envolver *m* wrapping paper
papel de escribir *m* writing paper
papel higiénico *m* toilet paper
paquete *m* packet
par *m* pair
para for
parabrisas *m* windscreen
parachoques *m* bumper
parada *f* stop

paraguas *m* umbrella
parar stop
parecer seem
parecerse resemble
parecido similar
pared *f* wall
pariente *m/f* relative
paro: en paro unemployed
parque *m* park
parrilla *f*: **a la parrilla** grilled
parte *f* part; **en otra parte**
  elsewhere; **en alguna parte**
  somewhere; **en todas**
  partes everywhere
pasado last; **poco pasado**
  rare; **pasado mañana** the
  day after tomorrow
pasajero *m* passenger
pasaporte *m* passport
pasar pass; overtake;
  happen; **¿qué pasa?** what's
  the matter?
pasatiempo *m* hobby
Pascua Easter
paseo *m* walk; **ir de paseo**
  go for a walk
pasillo *m* corridor
paso a nivel *m* level crossing
paso de peatones *m*
  pedestrian crossing
pasta *f* tea biscuit; pastry
pasta de dientes *f* toothpaste
pastel *m* cake
pastelería *f* cake shop
pastilla *f* tablet
pastillas para la garganta *fpl*
  throat pastilles
patata *f* potato
patatas fritas *fpl* chips; crisps
paté *m* pâté
patinar skid; skate
pato *m* duck
pavo *m* turkey

peatón *m* pedestrian; **zona**
  para peatones *f* pedestrian
  precinct
pecho *m* chest; breast
pedal *m* pedal
pedazo *m* piece
pedir order; ask for
peine *m* comb
pelea *f* fight
película *f* film; **película en**
  color colour film
peligro *m* danger
peligroso dangerous
pelo *m* hair
pelota *f* ball
peluquería *f* hairdresser's
pendientes *mpl* earrings
pene *m* penis
penicilina *f* penicillin
pensar think
pensión *f* guesthouse;
  media pensión half board;
  pensión completa full
  board
pensionista *m* old-age
  pensioner
peor worse; worst
pepino *m* cucumber
pequeño small
pera *f* pear
percha *f* coathanger
perder lose; miss
perdón, perdone sorry;
  excuse me; pardon
perezoso lazy
perfecto perfect
perfume *m* perfume
periódico *m* newspaper
periodo *m* period
permanente *f* perm
permiso *m* licence
permitido allowed
permitir allow

pero but
perra f: **no tengo una perra** I'm broke
perrito caliente m hotdog
perro m dog
persona f person
pesadilla f nightmare
pesado heavy
pesar weigh
pesca f fishing
pescadería f fishmonger's
pescado m fish
peso m weight
pez m fish
picadura f bite
picante hot; spicy
picar sting; itch
picnic m picnic
picor m itch
pie m foot; **a pie** on foot
piedra f stone
piel f skin; **abrigo de pieles** m fur coat
pierna f leg
pijama m pyjamas
pila f battery
píldora f pill
piloto m pilot
pimienta f pepper (*spice*)
pimiento m pepper (*red, green*)
pincel m paint brush
pinchazo m puncture
pintar paint
pinza de la ropa f clothes peg
pinzas fpl tweezers
piña f pineapple
pipa f pipe
piragua f canoe
piscina f swimming pool
primer piso m first floor
piso m floor; flat

pistola f gun
plancha f iron
planchar iron
plano flat
plano m map
planta f plant
planta baja f ground floor
plástico m plastic
plata f silver
plátano m banana
platillo m saucer
plato m plate
playa f beach
playeras fpl trainers
plaza f square
pluma f pen
pobre poor
poco little; **pocos** a few
poder: puedo/ puede I/ he can
policía f police
policía m policeman
política f politics
político political
polo m ice lolly
polvo m powder; dust
pollo m chicken
pomada f ointment
pomelo m grapefruit
poner put
poney m pony
poquito m: **un poquito** a little bit
por by; through; for; **por semana** per week; **por allí** over there
por ciento per cent
por favor please
por qué why
porque because
portero m porter; doorman
posible possible
postal f postcard

SPANISH-ENGLISH

poster *m* poster
postre *m* dessert
precio *m* price
preferencia *f* right of way
preferir prefer
prefijo *m* dialling code
pregunta *f* question
preguntar ask
premio *m* prize
preparar prepare
presentar introduce
preservativo *m* condom
prestado: pedir prestado borrow
prestar lend
primavera *f* spring
primera (clase) *f* first class
primer, primero first
primeros auxilios *mpl* first aid
primo *m*, **prima** *f* cousin
princesa *f* princess
principal main
príncipe *m* prince
principiante *m* beginner
principio *m* beginning
prisa *f*: **darse prisa** hurry; **¡dese prisa!** hurry up!
privado private
probablemente probably
probar try
probarse try on
problema *m* problem
profesor *m*, **profesora** *f* teacher
profundo deep
programa *m* programme
prohibido forbidden
prometer promise
prometido engaged
prometido *m*, **prometida** *f* fiancé, fiancée
pronostico del tiempo *m* weather forecast
pronto soon
pronunciar pronounce
propietario *m* owner
propina *f* tip
propósito: a propósito deliberately
proteger protect
protestante Protestant
provecho: ¡buen provecho! enjoy your meal!
próximo next
prudente careful
público public
público *m* public; audience
pueblo *m* village
puente *m* bridge
puerro *m* leek
puerta *f* door; gate
puerto *m* harbour; pass
puesta del sol *f* sunset
pulga *f* flea
pulmones *mpl* lungs
pulmonía *f* pneumonia
pulpo *m* octopus
pulsera *f* bracelet
punto *m*: **hacer punto** knit
puro *m* cigar

que: más feo que uglier than; **la persona/ casa que** the person who/ house that; **pienso que ...** I think that ...
¿qué? what?
quedarse stay; **quedarse con** keep
quejarse complain
quemadura *f* burn

quemadura de sol *f* sunburn
quemar burn
querer love; want; **quisiera**
  I would like
querido dear
queso *m* cheese
¿quién? who?
quince días fortnight
quitaesmalte *m* nail polish
  remover
quizás maybe

radiador *m* radiator
radio *f* radio
radio *m* spoke
radiografía *f* X-ray
rama *f* branch
rápidamente quickly
rápido fast
raro rare; strange
rata *f* rat
ratón *m* mouse
razonable sensible
realmente really
rebajas *fpl* sale
rebanada *f* slice
recado *m* message
recepción *f* reception
recepcionista *m/f*
  receptionist
receta *f* recipe; prescription
recibo *m* receipt
recoger collect; pick up
recomendar recommend
reconocer recognize
recordar remember
recuerdo *m* souvenir
red *f* net; network
redondo round

reembolsar refund
refresco *m* soft drink
regalo *m* present
reina *f* queen
reír laugh
relajarse relax
religión *f* religion
reloj *m* watch; clock
remolque *m* trailer
reparar repair
repente: de repente suddenly
repetir repeat
representante *m/f* agent
repuestos *mpl* spare parts
repugnante disgusting
resaca *f* hangover
resbaladizo slippery
reserva *f* reservation
reservar reserve; book
resfriado *m* cold
respirar breathe
responder answer
responsable responsible
respuesta *f* answer
restaurante *m* restaurant
resto *m* rest
retraso *m* delay
retrovisor *m* rearview mirror
reumatismo *m* rheumatism
reunión *f* meeting
revelar develop
revisar check
revista *f* magazine
rey *m* king
rico rich
ridículo ridiculous
rímel *m* mascara
rincón *m* corner
riñón *m* kidney
río *m* river
robar steal
roca *f* rock
rock *m* rock music

rodilla *f* knee
rojo red
romper break
ron *m* rum
ropa *f* clothes
ropa de cama *f* bed linen
ropa interior *f* underwear
ropa sucia *f* laundry
rosa pink
rosa *f* rose
roto broken
rotulador *m* felt-tip pen
rubéola *f* German measles
rubio blond
rueda *f* wheel
rueda de repuesto *f* spare wheel
ruido *m* noise
ruidoso noisy
ruinas *fpl* ruins
ruta *f* route

S

sábado *m* Saturday
sábana *f* sheet
saber know; **no sé** I don't know
sabor *m* taste
sacacorchos *m* corkscrew
sacapuntas *m* pencil sharpener
sacar take out; get out
saco de dormir *m* sleeping bag
sal *f* salt
sala de espera *f* waiting room
salado salty
salchicha *f* sausage
sales de baño *fpl* bath salts

salida *f* exit; departure
salida de emergencia *f* emergency exit
salir go out
salmón *m* salmon
salsa *f* sauce
saltar jump
salud *f* health; **¡salud!** cheers!
saludos best wishes
sandalias *fpl* sandals
sandía *f* watermelon
sangrar bleed
sangre *f* blood
sano healthy
sarampión *m* measles
sardina *f* sardine
sartén *f* frying pan
se himself; herself; itself; yourself; oneself; yourselves; themselves; **se vende** for sale; **¿se puede fumar?** is smoking allowed? (*see grammar*)
secador de pelo *m* hair dryer
secar dry
seco dry
secreto secret
sed *f*: **tengo sed** I'm thirsty
seda *f* silk
seguir follow
segunda clase *f* second class
segundo *m* second
seguro safe; sure
seguro *m* insurance
sello *m* stamp
semáforos *mpl* traffic lights
semana *f* week
sencillo simple
sensible sensitive
sentar: sentar bien (a) suit
sentarse sit down
sentir feel; **me/ no me siento**

bien I feel well/ don't feel well
señal de tráfico *f* roadsign
señor *m* sir; **un señor** a gentleman, a man; **el señor Brown** Mr Brown
señora *f* madam; **una señora** a lady, a woman; **la señora Brown** Mrs Brown
señorita *f* miss; **una señorita** a young lady; **la señorita Brown** Miss Brown
separado separate; **por separado** separately
septiembre September
ser be (*see grammar*)
serio serious
servicio *m* service
servicios *mpl* toilet
servilleta *f* serviette
servir serve
si if; **si no** otherwise
sí yes; himself; herself; itself; oneself; yourself; yourselves; themselves; each other
SIDA *m* AIDS
sidra *f* cider
siempre always
siglo *m* century
significar mean
siguiente next
silencio *m* silence
silla *f* chair
silla de ruedas *f* wheelchair
sillita de ruedas *f* pushchair
sillón *m* armchair
simpático nice
sin without
sinagoga *f* synagogue
sincero sincere
sobre on; above
sobre *m* envelope

sobrina *f* niece
sobrino *m* nephew
sociedad *f* society
¡socorro! help!
sol *m* sun
soleado sunny
solo alone
sólo only
soltero single
soltero *m* bachelor
sombra *f* shade
sombra de ojos *f* eye shadow
sombrero *m* hat
somnífero *m* sleeping pill
sonreír smile
sopa *f* soup
sordo deaf
sorpresa *f* surprise
sótano *m* basement
su his; her; its; one's; your; their (*see grammar*)
suave soft
subir go up; get on/ in
suceder happen
sucio dirty
sudar sweat
suegra *f* mother-in-law
suegro *m* father-in-law
suela *f* sole
suelo *m* floor
suelto *m* change
sueño *m* dream; **tengo sueño** I'm sleepy
suerte *f* luck; **¡buena suerte!** good luck!
suéter *m* sweater
suficiente: es suficiente that's enough
Suiza *f* Switzerland
suizo Swiss
sujetador *m* bra
supermercado *m* supermarket

suplemento *m* supplement

supuesto: por supuesto of course

sur *m* south; **al sur de la ciudad** south of the town

sus his; her; its; one's; your; their (*see grammar*)

susto *m* shock

suyo, suya his; hers; its; yours; theirs (*see grammar*)

tabaco *m* tobacco

tabla *f:* **tabla a vela** sailboard

tablero de instrumentos *m* dashboard

tacón *m* heel

talco *m* talcum powder

talón *m* heel

talonario de cheques *m* cheque book

talla *f* size

también also; **yo también** me too

tampón *m* tampon

tan: tan bonito como as beautiful as; **tan bonito** so beautiful

tapa *f* lid

tapón *m* plug

taquilla *f* ticket office

tarde late

tarde *f* afternoon; evening; **buenas tardes** good evening; **a las 3 de la tarde** at 3 p.m.

tarjeta *f* card

tarjeta de banco *f* cheque card

tarjeta de crédito *f* credit card

tarjeta de embarque *f* boarding pass

tarta *f* cake; **tarta de manzana** apple pie

taxi *m* taxi

taza *f* cup

te you; yourself (*see grammar*)

té *m* tea

teatro *m* theatre

techo *m* ceiling

tejado *m* roof

tela *f* material

teleférico *m* cable car

teléfono *m* telephone

telegrama *m* telemessage

telesilla *f* chairlift

televisión *f* television

temperatura *f* temperature

temporada *f* season

temprano early

tenedor *m* fork

tener have; **¿tiene ...?** have you got ...?; **tengo/ tiene que** I/ he must; **tengo 25 años** I'm 25 years old

tenis *m* tennis

terminar finish

termo *m* thermos flask

termómetro *m* thermometer

ternera *f* veal

terrible terrible

testigo *m* witness

tetera *f* teapot

tía *f* aunt

tibio lukewarm

tiburón *m* shark

tiempo *m* time; weather; **a tiempo** on time

tienda *f* shop; tent

tienda libre de impuestos *f* duty-free shop

SPANISH-ENGLISH

tierra *f* earth
tijeras *fpl* scissors
timbre *m* bell
tímido shy
tinto red (wine)
tintorería *f* dry-cleaner's
tío *m* uncle
tirar pull; throw; throw away
tirita *f* sticking plaster
toalla *f* towel
tobillo *m* ankle
tocadiscos *m* record player
tocar touch
todavía still; **todavía no** not yet
todo (*adjective*) all; **todos los días** every day; (*pronoun*) everything; **todos** everyone
tomar take; **tomar el sol** sunbathe
tomate *m* tomato
tónica con ginebra *f* gin and tonic
torcer twist; sprain
tormenta *f* storm
tornillo *m* screw
toro *m* bull
torre *f* tower
tortilla *f* omelette
tos *f* cough
toser cough
tosferina *f* whooping cough
tostada *f* toast
total *m* total; **en total** altogether
trabajar work
trabajo *m* work; job
tradición *f* tradition
tradicional traditional
traducir translate
traer bring
tráfico *m* traffic

tragar swallow
traje *m* suit; dress
traje de baño *m* swimming costume
tranquilizarse calm down
tranquilo quiet
transmisión *f* transmission
trasero back
trasero *m* bottom
tren *m* train
tripulación *f* crew
triste sad
trueno *m* thunder
tu your (*see grammar*)
tú you (*see grammar*)
tubería *f* pipe
tubo de escape *m* exhaust
tuerca *f* nut
tumbona *f* deck chair
túnel *m* tunnel
turista *m* tourist
turno: es mi turno this round is on me
tus your (*see grammar*)
tuyo, tuya yours (*see grammar*)

U

último last
ultramarinos *m* grocer's
un a (*see grammar*)
una a (*see grammar*)
unas some; **unas flores** (some) flowers (*see grammar*)
universidad *f* university
uno one; someone (*see grammar*)
unos some; a few (*see grammar*)
uña *f* fingernail

SPANISH-ENGLISH

urgente urgent
usar use
Usted/ Ustedes you (*see grammar*)
utensilios de cocina *mpl* cooking ustensils
útil useful
uvas *fpl* grapes

vaca *f* cow
vacaciones *fpl* holiday
vacaciones de verano *fpl* summer holidays
vacío empty
vacuna *f* vaccination
vagina *f* vagina
vagón *m* carriage
vainilla *f* vanilla
vale OK
valer be worth
válido valid
valiente brave
válvula *f* valve
valla *f* fence
valle *m* valley
vapor *m* steamer
vaqueros *mpl* jeans
variable changeable
varios several
varonil macho; manly
Vd(s). you (*see grammar*)
vecino *m* neighbour
vegetariano vegetarian
vehículo *m* vehicle
vejiga *f* bladder
vela *f* candle; sail
velocidad *f* speed
velocímetro *m* speedometer
venda *f* bandage

vender sell
veneno *m* poison
venir come
venta *f* sale
ventana *f* window
ventilador *m* fan
ver see
verano *m* summer
verdad *f* truth; **¿verdad?** isn't it?, don't you? etc
verdadero true
verde green
verduras *fpl* vegetables
vestido *m* dress
vestir dress
vez *f* time; **una vez** once; **otra vez** again; **a veces** sometimes
viajar travel
viaje *m* journey; **¡buen viaje!** have a good journey!
viaje de negocios *m* business trip
viaje de novios *m* honeymoon
viaje organizado *m* package tour
vida *f* life
vídeo *m* video
viejo old
viento *m* wind
viernes Friday
vinagre *m* vinegar
vino *m* wine; **vino tinto/ blanco/ rosado** red/ white rosé wine
viñedo *m* vineyard
violación *f* rape
violento embarrassing
visado *m* visa
visita *f* visit
visitar visit
visor *m* viewfinder

SPANISH-ENGLISH

vista *f* view
vitaminas *fpl* vitamins
viuda *f* widow
viudo *m* widower
vivir live
vivo alive
volante *m* steering wheel
volar fly
volver come back; **volver a casa** go home; **volver a hacer** do again
vosotros, vosotras you (*see grammar*)
voz *f* voice
vuelo *m* flight
vuestro, vuestra your; yours (*see grammar*)

zapatillas *fpl* slippers
zapatos *mpl* shoes
zona *f* area
zoo *m* zoo
zumo *m* juice
zurdo left-handed

water *m* toilet

y and
ya already
ya que since
yerno *m* son-in-law
yo I; me (*see grammar*)
yogur *m* yoghurt

zanahoria *f* carrot
zapatero *m* cobbler

CONVERSION TABLES

metres
  1 metre = 39.37 inches or 1.09 yards

kilometres
  1 kilometre = 0.62 or approximately ⅝ mile

to convert kilometres to miles: divide by 8 and multiply by 5

kilometres:	2	3	4	5	10	100
miles:	1.25	1.9	2.5	3.1	6.25	62.5

miles
to convert miles to kilometres: divide by 5 and multiply by 8

miles:	1	3	5	10	20	100
kilometres:	1.6	4.8	8	16	32	160

kilos
  1 kilo = 2.2 or approximately 1⅕ pounds

to convert kilos to pounds: divide by 5 and multiply by 11

kilos:	4	5	10	20	30	40
pounds:	8.8	11	22	44	66	88

pounds
  1 pound = 0.45 or approximately 5/11 kilo

litres
  1 litre = approximately 1¾ pints or 0.22 gallons

Celsius
to convert to Fahrenheit: divide by 5, multiply by 9, add 32

Celsius:	10	15	20	25	28	30	34
Fahrenheit:	50	59	68	77	82	86	93

Fahrenheit
to convert Fahrenheit to Celsius: subtract 32, multiply by 5, divide by 9

THE DEFINITE ARTICLE (THE)

Spanish nouns are either masculine or feminine and so articles must have a different form depending on whether the noun is masculine, feminine, singular or plural:

	masculine	*feminine*
singular	**el**	**la**
plural	**los**	**las**

el hotel the hotel	**los hoteles** the hotels
la casa the house	**las casas** the houses

Note that **de** + **el** becomes **del** and **a** + **el** becomes **al**:

el café	**voy al café**	I'm going to the café
el hotel	**al lado del hotel**	beside the hotel

THE INDEFINITE ARTICLE (A, AN, SOME)

	masculine	*feminine*
singular	**un**	**una**
plural	**unos**	**unas**

un hombre a man	**unos hombres** (some) men
una cerveza a beer	**unas cervezas** (some) beers

NOUNS

Most nouns ending in **-o** are masculine. Most nouns ending in **-a**, **-ción**, **-d** or **-z** are feminine (although there are exceptions).

PLURALS are formed by following these rules:

Nouns ending in a vowel: add **-s**

singular	*plural*	
la casa	**las casas**	house/houses

Nouns ending in a consonant: add **-es**

el autobús	**los autobuses**	bus/buses

Nouns ending in **-z**: change **-z** to **-ces**

la luz	**las luces**	light/lights

GRAMMAR

ADJECTIVES normally come after the noun and 'agree' with it. The dictionary in this book gives the masculine form. To make the feminine form just carry out the following changes:

masculine	*feminine*
-o	**-a**
-or	**-ora**
-és	**-esa**
-ón	**-ona**

In most other cases masculine and feminine forms are the same:

| **un niño grande** | a big child |
| **una casa grande** | a big house |

The plurals of adjectives are formed just like the nouns:

masculine	*feminine*
grande	**grandes**
marrón	**marrones**

COMPARATIVES are formed by putting **más** in front of the adjective:

| **barato** | cheap |
| **más barato** | cheaper |

'Than' is **que**:

es más caro que el mío
it's more expensive than mine

'Less ... than' is **menos ... que**:

hace menos calor que ayer
it's less hot than yesterday

'As ... as' is **tan ... como**:

estoy tan morena como tú
I'm as suntanned as you

SUPERLATIVES are formed by putting **el más, la más, los más** or **las más** in front of the adjective:

	el más pequeño	
or	**la más pequeña**	
	the smallest	

	los más caros	
or	**las más caras**	
	the most expensive	

GRAMMAR

POSSESSIVE ADJECTIVES agree with their noun. They are:

	m sing	*f sing*	*m pl*	*f pl*
my	**mi**	**mi**	**mis**	**mis**
your (*fam**)	**tu**	**tu**	**tus**	**tus**
his/her/ its/				
your	**su**	**su**	**sus**	**sus**
our	**nuestro**	**nuestra**	**nuestros**	**nuestras**
your (*fam**)	**vuestro**	**vuestra**	**vuestros**	**vuestras**
their/ your	**su**	**su**	**sus**	**sus**

mi coche	my car
nuestro hotel	our hotel
vuestras amigas	your (girl)friends
su coche	his/her/ your/ their car

As you can see the meaning of **su** is not always clear. **Su** can be replaced by **de él/ de ella/ de Usted/ de ellos/ de ellas/ de Ustedes**:

el coche de él	his car
la maleta de ella	her suitcase
las maletas de Usted	your suitcases
el hotel de ellos	their hotel

* familiar form, see *YOU*.

DEMONSTRATIVE ADJECTIVES (THIS, THAT etc) are masculine or feminine depending on the gender of the noun. There are three:

este means this (near the speaker)
ese means that (near the person spoken to)
aquel means that (distant from both)

m sing	**este**	**ese**	**aquel**
f sing	**esta**	**esa**	**aquella**
m pl	**estos**	**esos**	**aquellos**
f pl	**estas**	**esas**	**aquellas**

ese vaso	that glass
estas maletas	these suitcases
aquellos chicos	those boys

ADVERBS are formed by adding **-mente** to the feminine form of an adjective:

verdaderamente	really
rápidamente	fast

GRAMMAR

PRONOUNS

	subject		direct object
yo	I	me	me
tú	you	te	you
él	he	le	him
ella	she	la	her
ello	it	lo/la	it
Usted	you	le/la	you
nosotros/as	we	nos	us
vosotros/as	you	os	you
ellos	they	les	them
ellas	they	las	them
Ustedes	you	les/las	you

	indirect object		reflexive
me	to me	me	myself
te	to you	te	yourself
le	to him	se	himself
le	to her	se	herself
		se	itself
le	to you	se	yourself
nos	to us	nos	ourselves
os	to you	os	yourselves
les	to them	se	themselves
les	to you	se	yourselves

Subject pronouns are not always used in Spanish:

vivo	can only mean	I live
comemos	can only mean	we eat

But the pronoun is used to avoid confusion or for emphasis:

yo no conozco Madrid – yo sí
I don't know Madrid – I do

After prepositions use the subject pronoun but change **yo** to **mí** and **tú** to **ti**:

para ella/ él/ Usted	for her/ him/ you
para mí/ ti	for me/ you

with **con** which means 'with' you say:

	con él/ con Usted	with him/ with you
but:	**conmigo/ contigo**	with me/ with you

GRAMMAR

Note the positioning of pronouns:

> **¿puede ayudarme?** — can you help me?
> **no le/te vi** — I didn't see him/you
> **me lo dio** — he gave it to me

YOU can be expressed in two ways in Spanish:

tú (*sing*) and **vosotros** (*plural*) are used in an informal way to address friends, relatives and children. They are also used between young people. They take the second person of the verb:

> **¿quieres bailar conmigo?**
> do you want to dance with me?

Usted (*sing*) and **Ustedes** (*plural*) are more formal. They are used to address people you don't know very well or people you would normally address by their surname. The third person of the verb is used with this form (ie the same as for 'he/she'):

> **¿cómo se llama Usted?** — what is your name?

POSSESSIVE PRONOUNS

	m sing	*f sing*	*m pl*	*f pl*
mine	el mío	la mía	los míos	las mías
yours (*fam*)	el tuyo	la tuya	los tuyos	las tuyas
his/hers/ yours	el suyo	la suya	los suyos	las suyas
ours	el nuestro	la nuestra	los nuestros	las nuestras
yours (*fam*)	el vuestro	la vuestra	los vuestros	las vuestras
theirs/ yours	el suyo	la suya	los suyos	las suyas

DEMONSTRATIVE PRONOUNS have masculine and feminine forms like the demonstrative adjectives but are written with an accent:

éste	**ése**	**aquél**
this one	that one	that one (over there)

There is also a neuter form for each one:

esto	**eso**	**aquello**
¿qué es esto?	what is this?	
eso es imposible	that's impossible	

GRAMMAR

VERBS in Spanish fall into three groups with **-ar**, **-er** and **-ir** endings. The *PRESENT TENSE* is formed by removing the **-ar**, **-er**, **-ir** and adding the following:

	hablar	*comer*	*vivir*
I	**habl-o**	**com-o**	**viv-o**
you (*fam*)	**habl-as**	**com-es**	**viv-es**
he/she/you	**habl-a**	**com-e**	**viv-e**
we	**habl-amos**	**com-emos**	**viv-imos**
you			
(*pl fam*)	**habl-áis**	**com-éis**	**viv-ís**
they/ you	**habl-an**	**com-en**	**viv-en**

¿dónde vives?	where do you live?
hablo un poco de español	I speak a bit of Spanish
comen en un restaurante	they eat in a restaurant

Some common verbs are irregular in the present tense:

tener (have)	*ir* (go)
tengo	**voy**
tienes	**vas**
tiene	**va**
tenemos	**vamos**
tenéis	**vais**
tienen	**van**

ser (be)	*estar* (be)
soy	**estoy**
eres	**estás**
es	**está**
somos	**estamos**
sois	**estáis**
son	**están**

There are two verbs for 'to be' in Spanish:

SER is used to indicate a permanent state or quality. It is used with occupations, nationalities and also expressions of time:

soy escocés	I'm Scottish
mi padre es médico	my father is a doctor
eres muy guapa	you are very beautiful
es difícil	it's difficult

GRAMMAR

ESTAR is used to indicate position or temporary states or conditions:

están en la playa	they are on the beach
¿estás cansado?	are you tired?

Some verbs are irregular in the first person only:

saber	know	**sé**	I know
hacer	do	**hago**	I do
dar	give	**doy**	I give
salir	go out	**salgo**	I go out

With *REFLEXIVE* verbs like 'llamarse' or 'levantarse' use the pronouns as listed under the section on pronouns:

me llamo ...	my name is ...
¿cómo te llamas?	what's your name?
nos levantamos a las ...	we get up at ...

The *IMPERFECT TENSE* is used to express what was going on or what someone was doing or used to do over an indefinite period of time. The endings are:

I	**habl-aba**	**com-ía**	**viv-ía**
you (*fam*)	**habl-abas**	**com-ías**	**viv-ías**
he/she/you	**habl-aba**	**com-ía**	**viv-ía**
we	**habl-ábamos**	**com-íamos**	**viv-íamos**
you (*pl fam*)	**habl-abais**	**com-íais**	**viv-íais**
they/you	**habl-aban**	**com-ían**	**viv-ían**

todos los días comíamos en el restaurante
we used to eat in the restaurant every day

There are only two irregular verbs in the imperfect tense:

	ser	*ir*
I	**era** (was)	**iba** (went)
you (*fam*)	**eras** (were)	**ibas**
he/she/you	**era**	**iba**
we	**éramos**	**íbamos**
you (*pl fam*)	**erais**	**ibais**
they/you	**eran**	**iban**

GRAMMAR

The **PAST HISTORIC** is used to express what happened or what somebody did at a particular time. The endings are:

I	habl-é	com-í	viv-í
you (*fam*)	habl-aste	com-iste	viv-iste
he/she/you	habl-ó	com-ió	viv-ió
we	habl-amos	com-imos	viv-imos
you (*pl fam*)	habl-asteis	com-isteis	viv-isteis
they/you	habl-aron	com-ieron	viv-ieron

el año pasado vivieron en Madrid
last year they lived in Madrid

The **FUTURE TENSE** (I will/shall) is formed by adding the following endings to **-ar**, **-er** or **-ir**:

I	hablar-é
you (*fam*)	hablar-ás
he/she/you	hablar-á
we	hablar-emos
you (*pl fam*)	hablar-éis
they/you	hablar-án